WARM-CLIMATE GARDENING

TIPS, TECHNIQUES, PLANS, PROJECTS FOR HUMID OR DRY CONDITIONS

by Barbara Pleasant

A Garden Way Publishing Book

STOREY

Storey Communications, Inc.
Schoolhouse Road
Pownal, Vermont 05261

Edited by Gwen W. Steege
Cover and text design by Meredith Maker
Text production by Nancy Bellnier, Mass Media
Cover photograph copyright © by William D. Adams
Line drawings by Brigita Fuhrmann
Indexed by Nan N. Badgett, Wordability

Garden Way Publishing was founded in 1973 as part of the Garden Way Incorporated Group of Companies, dedicated to bringing gardening information and equipment to as many people as possible. Today the name "Garden Way Publishing" is licensed to Storey Communications, Inc., in Pownal, Vermont. For a complete list of Garden Way Publishing titles call 1-800-827-8673. Garden Way Incorporated manufactures products in Troy, New York, under the Troy-Bilt® brand including garden tillers, chipper/shredders, mulching mowers, sicklebar mowers, and tractors. For information on any Garden Way Incorporated product, please call 1-800-345-4454.

Printed in the United States by The Book Press
First Printing, February, 1993

Library of Congress Cataloging-in-Publication Data

Pleasant, Barbara.
    Warm-climate gardening : tips, techniques, plans, projects for humid or dry conditions / Barbara Pleasant.
              p.   cm.
      Includes index.
      ISBN 0-88266-819-6 (hc) — ISBN 0-88266-818-8 (pbk.)
      1. Gardening — Sunbelt States.   I. Title.
    SB453.2.S86P58   1993
    635.9'52 — dc20   92-54255
                                 CIP

CONTENTS

INTRODUCTION

WARM-CLIMATE GARDENERS DON'T MAKE JOKES about okra. We have no trouble seeing beauty in a cactus, and we love shade. Few of us plant more in May than we do in September, and most of us wonder how anyone could have trouble growing a tomato.

This book is about these and the thousand other ways that gardening in warm climates is different from mainstream gardening, which somehow has been defined by how plants are grown in England and the northeastern United States. But what works in London won't work in Atlanta, and, horticulturally speaking, Boston and Phoenix have very little in common.

No matter where you live, gardening smart means working with nature to help plants grow. If you live in a warm climate, this book will help you pick up the right planting rhythms, choose the best plants, and discover useful techniques to make your gardening easier and more rewarding.

For lack of better terminology, I often refer to winter hardiness zones as defined and updated by the U.S. Department of Agriculture (USDA) in 1990. These zones are meant to estimate winter hardiness, and the warmest ones break down like this:

Zone	Average Minimum Temperature
10	30°F to 40°F
9	20°F to 30°F
8	10°F to 20°F
7	0°F to 10°F

Since these zones incorporate no information about summer temperatures or rainfall patterns, their only appropriate use is for estimating winter hardiness. There is no such thing as a summer hardiness map, but here's a tip that works well throughout the year. Designate your own zone range by using the numbers just above and below the zone where you live. For example, if you live in Zone 7, figure on needing a range of 6 to 8; in Zone 8, look for 7 to 9. When looking at a plant you want, note whether it bears a zonal rating — like "grows well in Zones 5–9" — fits within your prescribed range.

Because I think gardening should be fun rather than frustrating, most of the suggested plants in this book have well deserved reputations for dependable performance where summers are hot and pests are many. Common names are used alone as much as possible, but in situations where you will need a botanical name to make the best plant choice, it is included.

I hope this book is of special use to new gardeners and people who have moved south after developing substantial gardening skills in other regions. Perhaps you never dreamed you would be growing chayote, but now you want to know how it's done. Or maybe you want perennial flowers, and most of the ones you have tried promptly died. Use *Warm-Climate Gardening* to solve problems like these before they happen. Along the way, I hope you find many ways to enjoy gardening more while working a little less.

Chapter One

A WALK THROUGH A WARM-CLIMATE GARDEN

THERE IS NO BETTER WAY to get acquainted with the rhythms and reasons behind warm-climate gardening than to walk through a few dozen of them to see how it is done. No two gardens are alike, but in my invasions into the private backyard worlds of gardeners, I have found that the best ones have one common characteristic: the gardeners themselves have an adventurous attitude. In warm climates, you never know when you'll have a wet year or a dry one, a mild summer or a scorcher, a treacherous winter or a sweet and easy one. Accomplished warm-climate gardeners appreciate these possibilities and align their gardening passions accordingly. They are always trying new plants, and new ways to grow them, in search of strategies that work.

This chapter tells you how to grow healthy, happy garden plants. We'll begin with how warm-climate gardeners approach the big four of gardening: composting, mulching, crop rotation, and pH monitoring. Then we'll look at custom methods many warm-climate gardeners use, and I'll share some of the best innovative ideas I've picked up from my visits with generous gardeners.

COMPOST

Every gardener should have a compost heap that gobbles up kitchen waste (vegetable trimmings and leftovers the dog won't eat), along with weeds and plant material from the garden.

In warm climates, compost is best thought of as medicine, or a health tonic, for tired soil. It works best when used as a preventive measure rather than a cure.

Compost is not normally rich in nitrogen, but it's full of fungi and bacteria. These organisms compete with and antagonize other microbes they encounter, while giving off enzymes and minerals plants can use. Every plant you grow can use a handful of compost blended into the soil around its roots. Finished compost can also be steeped into a tea to spray on plants afflicted with foliar diseases. (See page 185 for details.)

It takes a few months to get a good compost heap going, whether the material is within the confines of some sort of composting appliance or sitting on the ground, preferably somewhere in the shade. Before a heap can work, it must become an established habitat for the talented microorganisms that cause things to rot. You furnish the setup, and these microorganisms do the work.

The setup does not have to be an exact mix of anything, but it must be a mix — of materials such as grass clippings, weeds, leaves, kitchen waste, and manure, all very well dampened. To kick-start a new heap, you can add special ingredients such as commercial compost activators, kelp meal, or soybean-based dog food. Once you have an established microorganism colony within your control, alll you have to do is put some of the compost from an old heap into a new heap, and you are on your way. Making compost is somewhat like making sourdough bread — you should always keep a starter culture on hand, ready to inoculate new batches.

After the raw materials, the next most important dimension of compost is water. Moisture mysteriously disappears from compost as it matures, so water must be constantly added. Covering an open heap with burlap bags can help slow moisture loss, but the microorganisms that live beneath will still be using a lot of water. Always locate your heap within convenient squirting distance of a faucet and wet new materials thoroughly as you add them. Enclosed composting appliances are great, but they often require daily watering during the warmest months.

If you were in the composting business, you would need to monitor your heap's temperature closely, since compost is not technically finished until it has heated up to over 100°F. Your backyard compost may never heat up very much, and you can look forward to many surprises when you use the com-

---

WEEDS IN YOUR COMPOST?

Whenever you suspect that a batch of compost is very weedy, use it for making compost tea (see page 185) or bury it deep beneath transplants, where sunlight won't invite the weed seeds to sprout and grow. Don't sterilize or solarize it, for much of compost's magic comes from living things that are easily killed by very high temperatures.

THE MANY MOODS OF MANURE

It has been said that the best fertilizer for any soil is its owner's footsteps, but I think manure is better. You can add manure directly to your soil or, better yet, mix it into your compost. Composting will get rid of some weed seeds (and possibly unwanted chemicals) in the manure, while vastly improving the speed and quality of the compost.

If you live in the city, check newspaper want ads for farmers who want to sell their manure. In the country, start talking to your neighbors, and eventually you'll find a convenient source. In either case, here are some material matters to consider.

Poultry manure is usually a combination of chicken doo and sawdust or peanut hulls. It is incredibly aromatic after it gets wet, but also very rich in nitrogen and other plant nutrients. If the manure comes from commercial broiler houses, it will have very few weed seeds. It is inexpensive, sometimes free.

Horse manure quality depends on what the animals eat. If they are fed some grain and the pasture they graze in mostly comprises forage grasses (rather than weeds), the manure will be moderately rich and very easy to work with. Stable managers often welcome manure gatherers. Well-trampled manure that has never been wet is easy to transport in heavy-weight plastic garbage bags.

Steer manure is mildly rich as manures go, but it is a valuable source of organic matter (basically, it's animal-processed grass). This type of manure is cheap and widely available in the West. Choose bags that have been kept dry, as they're lighter and easier to handle.

Cow or hog manure is quite variable, and much of what farmers sell has been taken from manure pits or lagoons. The consistency is, therefore, gloppy, but the nutrient content is high, and the manure will be a valuable addition to the compost heap.

Bat and cricket manure have high concentrations of nitrogen and are best used as strong fertilizers. It can be added to compost, but it's more economical to use these special manures for top-dressing growing plants that need a little boost.

post for any aboveground use. Squash, pumpkin, tomato, and annual vinca seeds survive composting very well. Indeed, I suspect that it is impossible to kill pumpkin seeds in a compost heap. When you see a pumpkin vine sprawling through a flower bed or tomatoes popping up among daylilies, you can be fairly certain that the property is managed by a composter.

People like to make up a lot of rules about composting, but this has more to do with human nature than with the nature of compost. They say not to include greasy things such as french fries, sweet things such as moldy pie, or raw meat such as dead mice. Phooey. Your only obligation when composting is not to offend yourself or anyone else. In truth, you can put just about anything into an established compost mix, provided you bury it deep down. Of course, you wouldn't want to make a habit of putting fatty, stinky stuff in there, or it will make your compost fatty, stinky, and full of flies.

Finally, compost must be turned, or somehow fluffed up, from time to time to keep air incorporated in the mix. If putrid odors waft your way as you turn

MULTI-PILE COMPOSTING

After years of experimentation, the composting system that works best for me consists of a series of four piles laid out side by side, so close that they almost overlap.

At the far end, very rough stuff (whole plants, limbs, and the like) is piled until is it brittle enough to be pulverized by stomping on it. At the other end is a stockpile of filler, bulky material such as leaves and grass clippings. In between, I generally have two piles that I turn back and forth on top of each other as new material (including manure) is added. To keep dogs and other animals from digging out the kitchen waste, I keep the pile with the newest material in a wire enclosure. A shovel is permanently stationed in the compost area.

the heap, you probably waited a little too long to aerate it. Compost that is turned regularly seldom smells bad, and it also works faster than compost that is compacted and airless inside.

Accept from the start that you will never have enough compost. Dole it out thoughtfully, and always make new to replace the old. Use extra compost when preparing soil for plants that stay in the ground for a long time, such as tomatoes and peppers. If you ever feel compelled to cheat on rotations (see pages 8-9), use a double portion of compost to help atone for this sin.

MULCHING

Each gardener must handle mulch as he or she sees fit, but you must handle it. A Cooperative Extension agent in Florida once told me that nothing would grow there without mulch. In Florida, as in many warm climates, the soil is too thin and the sun too hot for plants to thrive without some type of surface insulation.

Some folks like to stick with leaves, gathered from curbside in garbage bags, which are piled together (often still in the bags) until they are needed. Others listen for the sound of tree-trimming crews cleaning up around power lines. Ask and you will usually receive a nice load of wood chips — provided you have a convenient place for them to be dumped.

I am partial to grass clippings, although I admit they sometimes smell like old diapers and must be set free from garbage bags immediately or they will turn into major yuck. Now that chemically treated lawns must have little signs posted on them for the first day or so after treatment, it's easy to tell whether the clippings may be contaminated with herbicides or other unwanted chemicals. I do not gather grass clippings during the second half of the summer, when they are most likely to contain seeds of common Bermuda grass or other obnoxious plants. The best grass clippings of the year are available in the spring, when they are likely to contain the most nitrogen, and in the fall, when the grass is often mixed with shredded leaves.

Leaves, wood chips, and grass clippings are free, but you can also buy your mulch. Straw (which is different from hay) is wonderful stuff and is especially valuable on sloping land where erosion is a problem. Hay contains so many weed seeds that you may want to pass it up. Shredded bark, available at garden centers in bulk or in bags, is quick and convenient to use, and it lends a neat appearance to high-visibility flower beds.

Whatever mulch you use, you will quickly become addicted to its miraculous powers to hold soil moisture, smother weeds, and enrich the soil with organic matter. As a general rule of thumb, mulches work best when they are about 2 inches thick after they have been compacted by rain. If you happen to be using a material that rots slowly and may tie up nitrogen temporarily, such as sawdust or wood chips, restrict its use to walkways or the top layer of a double mulch.

In flower beds and among vegetables like peppers and tomatoes that stay in the ground all summer, you may need to use a double mulch to get good full-season weed control. I like to use a layer of thickly folded newspaper covered with grass clippings or something else that will rot. Black or brown plastic overlaid with an organic mulch works well, too, but do remember to perforate the plastic with small holes or slits to allow the passage of water, and make sure you mulch over it so deeply that sunshine cannot reach the plastic to degrade it. If you use very heavy plastic as an

BUGGY MULCHES

If you live in a desert area where all living things are constantly seeking shelter from the sun, insects and small animals may find your mulch irresistible. Keep a sharp eye out for problems and be prepared to compost a mulch that becomes overrun with plant-eating insects. Short of going mulchless, invite predators such as frogs, lizards, and friendly snakes (if you can stand their slithery company) to keep down the bugs.

undermulch and take it up at the end of autumn, it may last two years or more.

With all types of mulch in all situations, remember to dampen the ground thoroughly before you mulch. A mulch does restrict the entry of rainfall a bit, but once the water is in the ground, the mulch will help keep it there.

ROTATIONS

In warm climates, the growing season is a series of short seasons that often overlap. It is not unusual for a vegetable gardener to plant three or four crops in the same plot each year, or for a flower gardener to turn over a front-yard bed three times. For example, last year one of my flower beds started out in petunias, went into multicolored sunflowers in midsummer, and was filled with pansies, chrysanthemums, and ornamental kale in the fall. In the vegetable garden, a certain trellis supported shell peas in late winter, cucumbers in spring, and a half-runner field pea in summer. By fall, it deserved a restorative cover crop.

For a crop turnover to be a good one, plant families should always be rotated, or mixed up in space and time, so that pests that require the presence of certain plants cannot gain a foothold. When you plant the same species in the same soil over and over, you are setting the stage for big problems with insects and soil-borne diseases.

The classic advice on rotations is never to follow plants of one family with plants of the same family. For this to work, you have to get to know the following families:

> **Brassicaceae** — cabbage, broccoli, leafy greens
>
> **Cucurbitaceae** — cucumbers, squash, melons
>
> **Leguminosae** — peas, beans
>
> **Solanaceae** — tomatoes, potatoes, peppers, eggplant
>
> **Umbelliferae** — carrots, parsley

Because rotations are so intense in warm climates, overly meticulous planning leads to confusion. I have the best luck flowing from season to season, using these simple guidelines to decide what to plant where:

* Group plant families together to make rotations easier to execute.

* When in doubt, plant a legume (bush beans, crowder peas, shell peas, soybeans, etc.).

* When rotations seem weak and you feel a planting is at risk, add an extra dollop of compost to the planting site.

* Whenever soil will not be used for six weeks or more, cover it with mulch or plant a cover crop.

For more ideas on how to implement rotations in your vegetable garden, see "Long-Season Succession Cropping" on page 63.

CLEVER COVER CROPS

No discussion of rotations would be complete without mention of the glue that holds rotations together: cover crops. There are always short periods of time when it's too late to plant one crop and not quite time to plant another. These are the "time windows" to look for, open, and put to good use with cover crops.

Depending on the season, you might choose any of a dozen cover crops, or perhaps a mixture of different things. I often use the tail-end contents of seed packets for cover crops. So what if the row is a jumble of field peas, bush beans, turnip greens, and marigolds! There is something growing there that's not a weed, and I can turn it under whenever the mood strikes me.

The choice of a cover crop varies with the season. For instance, if you choose legumes (which add nitrogen to the soil if turned under just before they flower), you could grow Austrian winter peas in winter, shell peas in spring, soybeans in early summer, field peas in late summer, and either clover or a mixture of leftovers in fall.

Grassy cover crops do a wonderful job of adding organic matter to the soil, although they are somewhat bulky to turn under, since they never winter-kill the way they do in cold climates. I use annual rye from fall to early spring, but instead of letting the plants reach full size, I turn them under while they are still young and tender. The same goes for cereal rye and wheat, which become very tough if allowed to grow for more than a couple of months. In summer, corn and sorghum make good cover crops, but again they are most manageable if turned under before they reach adolescence. When you turn under any cover crop when young, you can usually recultivate and replant the space in two to three weeks, provided the weather cooperates with your plan.

A few seed companies sell seasonal blends of cover crop plants that are nifty to use. A cover crop often can be planted alongside other crops that are nearing their zenith so that both crops can be turned under at the same time. This is called undercropping. For example, when hot weather is right around the corner in spring, why not let a few soybeans fill in vacant spaces until the lettuce bed is ready for renovation? Alfalfa attracts whiteflies in my garden, but if it hosts no pests in yours, it can be a wonderful undercrop for flowers, brassicas, or beans.

I use cover crops a lot, as my experience transforming compacted slime into good soil taught me that it's the easiest way to loosen and enrich dead dirt. Living plants do something magical for soil that manure and other soil amendments simply can't. To me, they recombine soil elements into ever more desirable patterns in a cycle that's seamlessly smooth and impossible to resist.

pH and Salt Monitoring

Now we get to something technical but simple, and very important. pH refers to the acidity of soil, which is rated numerically. Most garden plants prefer a nearly neutral pH of 5.5 to 6.0 but can tolerate a range of 5.0 to 6.5. If you get lower than 5.5, things are getting too acidic. Above 6.5, you're too alkaline. If your soil pH is too extreme in either direction, plants will have difficulty taking up nutrients, will not grow well, and will not be able to respond to challenges from pests. Inexpensive soil pH test kits are available at most garden centers. Unless everything is growing perfectly in your garden, it's a good idea to check the pH every year or so.

Many soils in the Southeast tend to be too acidic. To raise the pH of acidic soils, work in a good dusting of agricultural lime in the fall at least every other year. Certain plants, such as clematis vines and wallflowers, may need additional lime around their roots. Other plants, such as blueberries, azaleas, and strawberries, thrive in acidic soils, so you may want to withhold lime from them.

In the West, many soils are too alkaline, meaning the pH is too high. The addition of organic matter can help, especially materials that are naturally acidic, such as rotten leaves, sawdust, and peat moss. You also can try adding a bit of sulfur to help bring down your pH. Never add lime to alkaline soil; it's the last thing you need.

Another soil problem often seen in the West is the buildup of salt in the soil. In desertlike conditions, groundwater holds a lot of salt. When you water your garden and the water evaporates, this salt is left behind in the soil. To slow down soil salinization, mulch heavily to limit the amount of evaporation that takes place, and keep your soil microbes active by using a lot of compost and rotted organic matter.

BE WARY OF WEEDS

Let's say you've done everything right: dug up your dirt, added the manure of your choice, started some compost cooking, and gathered so much mulch that every crevice in your car has caught bits of leaves, straw, or grass clippings. If you now plant some seeds and leave them alone for a couple of months, what will grow in your glorious garden? — weeds, those miraculous plants nature has provided to heal over the scars we make when we scratch open the surface of the earth.

Just as we warm-climate gardeners can grow a long succession of vegetables and flowers, we also can grow bodacious crops of weeds. There are warm-season weeds for summer, cool-season weeds for fall, and many biennial and stump-rooted perennial weeds that like nothing better than to colonize enriched garden soil. Weeds are always there — you can never get rid of them — but it's not that hard to control them. You just have to work at it.

Do you have to hoe down, pull up, or mulch over every last weed? If your garden is small, why not? Every weed plant is taking up space, moisture, and soil resources that could be put to better use. In a large garden, strict weed control can get to be too much work. When I had a quarter-acre vegetable garden to tend, I found it was better to make friends with certain weeds and accept their presence than to wage an ongoing war with every last one of them.

One of the weeds I came to like after a while was red-rooted pigweed (a species of *Amaranth*) that makes a fine companion for tomatoes, since blister beetles and flea beetles often eat it instead of, or at least before, the tomatoes. The pigweed also smothered out other weeds, so I could let it get ankle high and then till it under as a wild cover crop.

I also learned to live with a wild vetch that was strong enough to outcompete other weeds and probably added some nitrogen to the soil. It attracted a lot of little wasps and other beneficial insects and made a nice cut flower. Watch closely how common weeds interact with the plants, insects, and soil in your garden, and you may find some friends among them too.

Besides making friends with certain weeds, there's the "if you can't beat 'em, join 'em" approach to weedy relationships. Over the years, whenever I have found desirable plants that reseed themselves without being overly aggressive about it, I have introduced them to the garden as substitutes for weeds. Several herbs — chamomile, oregano, and parsley — have worked well for me, although the success of these plants at naturalization is short-lived and the seed supply must be replenished every other fall. Various clovers seem to be a bit more persistent, especially when you let preferred clumps reseed.

The list of cultivated plants that make good weed competitors is long. Annual vincas are welcome weeds as far as I'm concerned, and I like to see volunteer marigolds and zinnias sprouting in unlikely places. Via composting, one of the most common weeds in my newer, scaled-down garden is the tomato. In spring I pull out tomato plants by the handful and throw them away — but not every last one. I save a few just to see what kinds of fruits develop, and over time I hope to have a private-issue strain of tomato, born and self-bred in my own backyard.

I hope you get the idea. The main reason for introducing selected weeds is to gain an edge against the ones you can't stand. Intolerable weeds include Bermuda grass, Johnsongrass, crabgrass, nutsedge, and any other rough, rangy plant that produces stout stolons (underground runners) or rhizomes (fat root pieces that sprout). Besides being more aggressive than any plants you are likely to grow, many superweeds have the uncanny ability to compact soil while exuding chemicals that poison other plants.

Vining weeds can be very hard to accept. Many nongardeners think that morning glories are beautiful, and they are. Yet after spending too many hot evenings trying to keep them from taking over my pole beans or plucking them out of tomato cages, I tell people never to plant them in a garden. If you must have morning glories (and they do grow like crazy in warm climates), put them in containers on a deck or patio and let them twine themselves around the structure. If your home borders an interstate highway, it might be a nice touch to plant them along the chain-link retaining fence.

No matter what you do, you can never get rid of every last weed. Weed seeds are always present in garden soil. Some stay viable for a decade or more, and every time the wind blows or a bird relieves itself over your soil, new weed seeds arrive. I visited a garden in Chattanooga that had been mulched thickly and continuously for twenty-five years with carefully selected straw, and it still had weeds. In another garden farther south, meticulous cover cropping with clover, soybeans, and rye had dramatically improved the soil, and weeds took advantage of the situation, growing quite rampantly.

I do have one good thing to say about weeds. Except for the most persistent ones, which should be laid out in the hot sun until they are crispy dead, weeds make good fodder for the compost heap. You can also use them as mulch. When you weed, simply shake the dirt from the roots and throw the whole plants beneath something that needs to be mulched. People often complain about weeding as being backbreaking work, but now that I have a small garden, I think it's a pretty cushy chore. I wait for a beautiful day, get out the dense foam pad I keep for this purpose, sit down where I can find a spot, and start weeding. By the time I'm finished, I've heard new birds singing, noticed some new details about how my plants and soil are growing, and made the bed look picture perfect. To me, weeding is among the most satisfying tasks a gardener can tackle.

TOOLS OF THE TRADE

Every gardener gradually accumulates a collection of tools that quickly become indispensable. But what do you really need? A tiller? A compost aerator? An imported aluminum-clad hand hoe with a leather-wrapped handle and a fifty-year guarantee?

I once created a new garden using no more than a shovel and a hoe, but I wouldn't do it again. To ease the labor, the following tools are basic equipment:

Shovel, for digging holes, turning soil, and moving compost and manure

Digging fork, for turning soil and compost heaps

Hoe, for leveling soil chunks and chopping out weeds

Leaf rake, for gathering leaves and pine straw

Dirt rake, for preparing seedbeds

Mattock, for breaking up compacted subsoil and chopping up raw compost

Hand trowel, for plugging in seedlings and digging out deep-rooted weeds

Hand rake, for weeding in tight places such as flower beds and mixing together buckets of compost, soil, and other planting materials

Wheelbarrow or cart, for moving stuff around

Couple of buckets, for picking produce and moving small amounts of compost and manure

Sturdy, hand-held clippers, for pruning and harvesting

Collection of gloves: What kind of gloves should you have? I suggest four different kinds: a heavy pair of work gloves for pruning and intense digging and hoeing, a lightweight pair for picking prickly things or light weeding, some good rubber gloves for handling chemicals (even the natural ones), and a box of surgical gloves (available at medical supply stores) for cutting up hot peppers and, if you're squeamish, squashing bugs.

In addition to these tools, many warm-climate gardeners regularly use several other devices to make their gardens easier to manage. Following are some of the items you might want to accumulate over time.

Tomato cages made from 6-inch-mesh concrete-reinforcing wire are great (see page 95 for directions on how to construct). Besides using them to provide support for tomatoes (especially the long, leggy indeterminate kinds), wire cages are wonderful compost catchers in the fall, when you need a place to dump accumulated leaves and dead plants. Open them out, and they can do double duty as arches that support plastic sheeting. Voila! Minigreenhouses. The wire arches also can hold up insulating blankets thrown over tender plants on cold nights. Arches can keep dogs and children away from freshly seeded areas and serve very well as trellises for cucumbers or dwarf peas. I have even grown cherry tomatoes on arches (as opposed to inside upright cages). Once the plants grew up through the arch, they sprawled happily and bore their fruits low, where my daughter and her little friends had no trouble picking them.

Many warm-climate gardeners also keep a few boards around, which come in very handy when you need to do some quick picking but you're wearing your good shoes. If you stand on the board, your footwear is protected from sole-seeping mud and dust. Boards also make nice anchors for the edges of sheet plastic or floating row cover and can be used to trap snails and slugs (which love to hide under boards in the daytime). A broad board will keep your behind clean if you sit on it while weeding and can be laid atop newly seeded beds in hot weather to help keep the seeds and soil moist for the first couple of days after planting.

You will also need a lot of flowerpots —plastic pots, clay pots, or whatever you can lay your hands on. Besides using them to grow plants, you can use them as shade covers over seedlings set out in hot or cold weather. Upside-down clay pots stay put in the wind, but plastic nursery liners will need to be weighted in place with a brick or large stone.

A final item to stash among your gardening supplies is a large tin can. I have found nothing better for scooping up potting soil or scattering wood ashes and lime.

I have enjoyed the use of three different tillers. With proper care and regular tune-ups, a tiller will last many years and shave hours off many gardening chores. Still, tilling is hard work, and you can save a lot of wear and tear on seldom-used arm and back muscles by tilling a little here and there rather than engaging in a weekend marathon. Also, wear earplugs when you till, for all tillers are noisy. Without ear plugs, cultivating a large garden is like going to a rock concert — at least as far as your ears are concerned.

With the basic stuff behind us, let's look at some of the special touches you are likely to see in great warm-climate gardens. These ideas and methods meet the climate halfway and make gardening more enjoyable and rewarding.

ROOMS WITH A VIEW

Just as you would not want every room in your house to be done up in the same colors or set the same mood, your yard should offer several different settings,

> ### DO YOU NEED A TILLER?
> How badly do you want one? How big is your garden? How much money do you have? If your garden is larger than 20 feet by 20 feet, you will certainly get good use out of a small tiller. Get one that is small enough for you to handle, and if you don't know a spark plug from a carburetor, find a talented repair person from the start.
>
> Tillers are extremely useful for a number of things, such as cultivating weeds, chopping up cover crops, preparing seedbeds, and incorporating soil conditioners, but they can't do everything. No tiller goes very deep (regardless of what the salesperson tells you). Even with the best tiller, you will still have to dig from time to time.

or microclimates, for different types of plants and gardening projects. Learning to recognize, enhance, and exploit these special places is a basic route to rewarding gardening.

For example, my yard has a dry, erodible bank, a cluster of trees, a morning-sun flower bed and another that sees the sun only in the afternoon, and a wide-open space out back for growing vegetables and a few fruits. The bank supports bulbs, wildflowers, and the beginnings of a dry rock garden. Selected flowers fill the beds, depending on how much shade they can take and how well they can resist diseases. Fruits fill the transition zone from shade to sun. The result is a flow of plants, each situated in a slightly different ecological niche.

To assess the potential of various parts of your yard, survey it carefully while looking for the following problem areas:

* **Are there any no-grow spaces dominated by big tree roots?** If you can find a planting pocket or two, perhaps a nice vine would add a touch of grace and sprawl enough to form a ground cover.

* **Do you have rocks beneath a skimpy cover of soil?** Try making a dry pond with more rocks, then stud it with flowers grown in hidden containers.

* **Does water pool up and refuse to drain?** Think in terms of streambed plants that like wet roots — irises, cannas, or even blueberries.

* **Does dry soil cook in the sun from dawn till dusk?** Start amending the soil with organic matter to help it hold water and explore permanent sources of shade, such as trees or a section of privacy fence.

* **Do you have a big swath of lawn that grows too well and requires constant mowing?** Don't waste it on grass! Where grass grows well, so will vegetables, herbs, and flowers.

THE BACKYARD NURSERY

The growing seasons in a warm-climate garden change and overlap, and in most places you can grow something all year long. But since you are continuously turning over plants, you should always have young plants ready to pop into the ground if old ones fail. Seedlings, rooted cuttings, and root divisions are just a few types of plants you might keep in a nursery bed — a special, protected place

where young plants can get the extra attention they need until they are strong
enough to make it in the outside world. Warm-climate
gardeners don't need just one
nursery bed; they need several. Following is a discussion
of the sites and schemes that have
worked best for me.

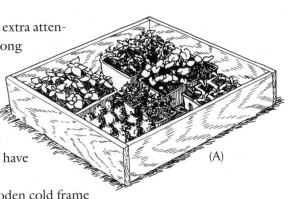

(A)

In early spring, I use a wooden cold frame
(A) covered with floating row cover instead of plastic or glass. (See the
directions for sewing one on page 37.) I keep the frame in full sun, with
containerized plants sitting directly on the ground
inside. When you top off your cold frame
with fabric row cover, you elimi-
nate overheating problems,
allow rainfall to enter, and
exclude flying insects,
while providing a warm, protected atmosphere for young plants.

In early summer, I move the nursery
to a place that gets only a few hours of midday
sun. To keep slugs and snails at bay, I set plants on
a wooden pallet. (B) This also discourages earthworms from entering the pots
and flats, which they love to do after a heavy rain.

(B)

In late summer, I move the nursery into a shallow trench (C) in a place that
gets only morning sun, with full shade in the afternoon. That way, I can water
the plants anytime but dur-
ing the late morning
hours without worrying
about burning tender
leaves. On a sunny day,
water on a leaf surface
may heat up to 140°F. Having
the containers below ground level
helps them hold water a little better,
while also keeping them cool.

(C)

By fall, the nursery bed needs to be moved out from under any trees, or it will be covered by falling leaves and the little plants may get bruised by acorns. My nursery area gets really big at this time of year, as I fill up dozens of containers, mostly old nursery liners, to start hardy perennials and annuals from seeds, or pot up divisions from plants that multiply into tight bunches. I keep these containers in full sun but very close to the faucet. (D) In fall, young containerized plants often need water every day.

In the winter, any nursery operation will do best in a place that offers some shelter from the north wind without blocking out too much sun. If you live where hard freezes are common, you may want to sink some containerized plants into the ground to limit heaving of the soil around the plants' roots. I let most of mine sit out unprotected and load them into the wheelbarrow and bring them into the garage if weather conditions get too terrible. (E)

Still, some situations call for an in-ground holding place for plants during the winter months. Plants that bunch during the cool weather, such as hardy alliums and perennial ornamental grasses, seem to do best down in the ground.

It's notable that I keep most, but not all, of my young plants in containers. This gives me a lot of flexibility in planting times and avoids the inevitable conflict with tree roots I encounter when I try to prepare a rich nursery bed near a tree. Tree roots find these soft, fertile spots easily and fill them up quickly. Three times I double-dug partially shaded beds in the spring, used them for a few months, and could not figure out why they stopped holding water in August. I got my answer when I dug up the beds in the fall. They were full of tree roots, which had no trouble absorbing the water I tried to give my struggling plants.

SHADY EXPOSURES

Part of the art of gardening in warm climates is learning to work effectively with light. You cannot rely on directives given in books or on seed packets to plant in full sun, for very few plants grown in warm climates really want to live this way. Through experience you'll learn what types of light various plants need in your garden. Following are some of the things you may discover.

In winter, when days are short and temperatures are cool, most plants like full sun. Pansies, parsley, and other plants typically grown during the winter require no shade.

In spring, plants that like cool weather, such as peas and lettuce, will do fine in full sun for a while but will require some shade when the weather warms up and days get longer. Afternoon shade is best. An easy way to provide it is to plant corn, sunflowers, bachelor's- buttons, or some other medium-size to tall plants on the southwest side of the ones that need to be shaded.

In summer, most plants can use a midday break from the sun, but this can be hard to provide. Placing hills of tall corn or sunflowers at strategic points in the vegetable garden sometimes works, or you can garden intensively along any edge of the garden that gets a bit of shade from trees. Even tomatoes benefit from slight shade in midsummer. If midday shade is impossible, look for places where your favorite plants will get a break in the late afternoon.

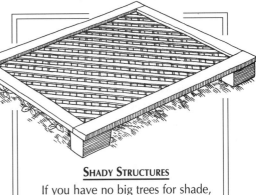

Sites that get morning shade are best for plants that are naturally adapted to shade. Morning shade postpones the drying of dew from plant leaves. Although moisture can be a contributing factor in the development of leaf spot diseases, plants that are naturally adapted to shady environments often have good

SHADY STRUCTURES

If you have no big trees for shade, use decorative wooden fences or overhead wooden trellises. Or use a slat house, a wooden structure with a roof made of widely spaced wooden slats that is placed over the garden. In the winter, it will do double duty as a greenhouse, covered with plastic. A simple wooden frame filled with lattice and propped up by bricks shades tender transplants.

defense mechanisms against these diseases. Common plants that grow naturally in partial shade, such as monardas, lilies, and impatiens, really like morning shade.

Sites that get morning sun and afternoon shade are the best places to try out new plants, grow perennials, or grow plants that have a temperate temperament. These are treasured spots to treat with respect. Enrich and exploit them! Create more by planting trees along the western perimeter of your property.

The important thing about light is to give it some serious thought. Learn to recognize plants' needs for both sun and shade and put both factors to good use. Approaches may be subtle, as when you plant corn alongside spring lettuce and spinach. Or you may use "bale beds," an idea passed on by a New Mexico gardener who grows her lettuce inside enclosures made from bales of hay. Light-altering devices such as arbors and trellises can add beauty to your yard while helping plants grow. I once saw a grapevine trained up a tall pole and across a wire to another pole, with various brambles planted beneath it. Working with shade often requires you to think in terms of multilevel planting — something for the high canopy and something lower that can use a bit of shade.

HOOP HOUSES

Where you need instant shade, as in a fall vegetable plot being planted with leafy greens and other cool-season plants, it's hard to beat a hoop house, covered with an old sheet or fabric shade cover like the ones nurseries use.

To build one 5 feet long, you will need three 4-foot sections of 1-inch-diameter flexible polyvinyl chloride (PVC) pipe and six 10-inch metal or wooden stakes narrow enough to stick into the ends of the pipe. Poke the stakes into the pipe pieces, and then arch the pipes over the bed and firm the stakes into place. Cover the pipes with fabric and secure the edges of the fabric with boards. The pipe hoops also can be used to support floating row covers (great protection from insects), sheet plastic (for quick spring warm-up), or netting to prevent birds from eating your crops.

BURIED BEDS

The earth often can be your best insulator against the drying effects of the sun. In summer, containerized plants, sunk down to the rim in soil, will be much happier than ones left sitting on the ground. Many plants will grow better in re-cessed trenches than in raised beds, since deep soil holds more water and is cooler than soil that sits up high. In

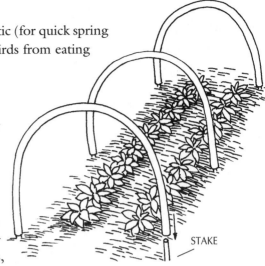

STAKE

A hoop house frame, consisting of PVC pipe and metal stakes

practice, you might grow summer vegetables in recessed pans — the opposite of raised beds. As the plants grow, you can move soil from the edges into the pan, which will give the plants a firm anchor to hold them in the wind, while also insulating them from the sun.

Historically, the idea of recessed plant-ing has been interpreted many different ways. In what is now the Southwest and Mexico, the Aztecs devised waffle beds, in which plantings were made in slightly excavated squares that caught water like little dishes. In Puerto Rico, early farmers made large bowls out of cultivated soil. They put plants that need a lot of water in the center and others that like things

Fabric shade cover supported by the frame and anchored with boards

dry along the edge. In the Southeast, rows of beans or corn are traditionally planted in furrows, and soil from between the rows is hoed up around the plants as they grow, forming a "dust mulch." American Indians had worked out this method by the seventeenth century.

More recently, innovative gardeners have discovered the value of lining garden beds to help keep the root zone moist and cool. Two gardeners I know have had success laying a lining of plastic beneath planting holes. The plastic acts as a subterranean barrier against moisture loss so that every drop of water you haul by hand really counts.

One fellow used this method for use with young blueberries, which need a lot of moisture (being lowland plants by nature). He also adds rotted sawdust to the planting site, and the combination of sawdust and subterranean plastic makes it possible for him to grow blueberries using only "heavy water" — the kind you have to bring in buckets from the nearest creek.

Another guy repeatedly tried to grow tomatoes in the only spot of sun on his woodland property, only to find that the site drained like a sieve. Finally, he laid a sheet of plastic beneath the tomato bed in early spring and poked several holes in it (just in case it turned out to be a very wet year). Thanks to the plastic and a wheelbarrowload of compost, he finally managed to grow the only crop he really wanted.

I have heard of several slightly different versions of this method, using everything from corncobs to newspaper as the underground lining. By all means, try these biodegradables, but bear in mind that they must never be allowed to dry out completely, or you will have a terrible time getting them soaking wet again. And don't forget to include some way for excess water to escape. You don't want to stop drainage completely; the goal is to stop surrounding superdry soil from wicking moisture away from the place where you want the water to stay.

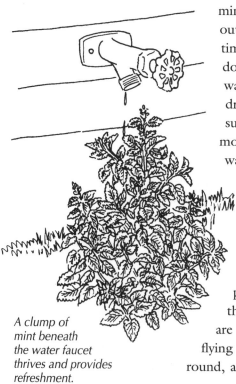

A clump of mint beneath the water faucet thrives and provides refreshment.

SMALL FEATURES

When I visit other people's gardens, I often use a tape recorder rather than trying to keep up with our spirited conversation with paper and pen. Upon playback, one of the first things I notice is the sound of birds. Warm-climate gardens are full of them, chirping, squawking, and flying about. Provide a water source year-round, and some millet and sunflower seeds in winter, to keep these music makers near your garden. They eat the bugs and are easily discouraged from pillaging your crops with bird netting (available at garden supply stores).

A lovely touch that used to be standard equipment in warm-climate gardens is a clump of mint beneath the water faucet. Mint is a vigorous, wonderful plant that loves the splattering it gets every time you use your hose. Best of all, when you wash up after working in the garden, you can grab a bunch, roll it between your hands, and experience the essence of freshness.

A PLACE FOR PEACE

In the hottest places on earth — the inhabited areas on the fringes of Africa's Sahara Desert — residents spend their evenings outdoors, sitting on little rugs in the sand, until their houses have a chance to cool down. Buildings are designed and situated so that they cast deep shadows, another way to provide people with passive shade.

In the Western Hemisphere's comparatively mild warm climates, we also need places where we can relax and wait for the sun to go down or the moon to come up. This peaceful place should be in or near the garden — a comfortable spot where you can sit and do nothing, or perhaps read, hum, or talk to the trees. It can be as plain as an upturned stump or as fancy as a Victorian gazebo.

The important thing is that it works well as a quiet place to experience the garden, which is every bit as important as growing it. What's the good of attracting butterflies and hummingbirds if you never take the time to watch them? Insights into how to solve gardening problems will never come to you unless you subject the situation to slow, contemplative study. In this way, a comfortable sitting spot can be as useful as a hoe.

I've been to a beautiful garden, nestled high in some remote hills, in which the sitting place was a lovely outhouse with no front door. Wisely, I think, the owner had built his outhouse to take advantage of the best view on his property, which included a rock garden in the foreground, a fruit orchard a little beyond that, and a hardwood forest with rolling hills in the distance.

Most of us have no need for outhouses, but we can help extend our homes out to the garden via shady decks, patios, pergolas, and old gazebos. If you have a nicely situated shade tree, a small garden bench underneath it will serve nicely. If you have no suitable trees, by all means consider a structure, such as a high, freestanding overhead trellis, or perhaps a pergola, added as an extension to

If you'd like a convenient place to stash your gloves, packets of seeds, trowels, and other small items, put up a mailbox at the garden's edge. It can save you numerous trips into the house (wearing muddy shoes) and keeps things from getting lost. You also can keep a small notebook and pencil there for jotting down varieties, planting dates, or the first appearance of a dreaded pest. The mailbox can do double duty as a trellis for a flowering or food-bearing vine.

your deck or patio for shade, shelter, and privacy. In the summer, these structures can support lush annual vines such as gourds or hyacinth beans; or, year-round, they can be clothed with the stems and foliage of perennial ornamental vines. Add a couple of chairs and a collection of container plants, and you have a tranquil outdoor retreat. Do install some type of low-maintenance "flooring," such as stones, bricks, or pebbles, for you don't want to have to mow and trim awkward nooks every other Saturday.

THE KIDS' CORNER

When your child reports excitedly, "Mama! The radishes are growing!" or asks hopefully, "Can we pick a bouquet?" his or her words are much more welcome than "Can I watch TV?" or "There's nothing to do." Kids love gardening, although they do have their own ideas about where to step, how to pick, and when to water and plant. For these reasons, it's a good idea to set aside a small plot of ground as the kids' corner. In my experience, all you have to do is prepare the soil and provide some seeds. From there, kids have an inborn talent for turning gardens into places of wonder.

For best results, select plants that bear many obvious things to pick — beans, pickling cucumbers, radishes, lettuce, and lots of flowers. Very little of this stuff will actually be eaten or displayed. Instead, it will end up stuck in pockets, collected in buckets, or picked and replanted in unlikely places.

Kids love water, and my top tip for keeping kids occupied in a garden is to give them a spray bottle, a squirt bottle, and a small watering can. On hot days, spritzing water here and there can keep them busy for a long time, and they will have fun doing it.

DUCKS AND CHICKENS

If you have a bit of space for a pen and no zoning restrictions to worry about, you might get a pair or ducks or a small flock of chickens to help you with your gardening. Ducks are the fowl of choice if you want help controlling insects, for they often can be allowed to roam around eating slugs and other bugs, especially if your property is fenced. Chickens eat bugs, too, but they also eat vegetables and flower seedlings. Chickens *near* the garden, where you can throw them old plants and collected bugs, are wonderful. Chickens *in* the garden, pecking up plants and shredding leaves into ribbons, are a nightmare.

Many gardeners keep their chickens in movable pens — wood and chicken-wire enclosures that can be lifted off the ground and moved to places that need to be cleaned of old plants and insects. As long as the birds have room to move around and interesting things to do, they seem quite happy in these contraptions.

SHARE IT WITH A FRIEND

There is one last thing you might want to bring into your garden from time to time. That thing is a person, any person, who seems curious, inspired, or somehow stimulated by what you are doing. Maybe it will be a child who never knew that potatoes are really roots or an older person who no longer has the strength to garden on his or her own. Or perhaps you will share your garden with a like-minded friend, if only for a little while. Gardening is a solitary business, but letting people into your gardening life can turn a bud of satisfaction into a vibrant flower of joy.

Chapter Two

GARDENING IN SIX SEASONS

BECAUSE THE GROWING SEASONS in warm climates are so long and varied, a visitor never sees but a slice of the garden's life in a single visit. At a garden in Chattanooga, for example, I saw long rows of sweet potatoes and pole beans in June, but not a trace of the spinach that was the gardener's pride and joy. Yet she had her planting rhythms right. Spinach has no place in a warm-climate garden in early summer, for it is not a warm-season crop.

In warm climates, the notion of "a growing season" is out of place. Rather, we operate within six strangely split seasons, with short transitional breaks in between. To help keep the pace and flow of warm-climate gardening in order, I've divided the year into six parts, as follows:

Winter: December through February

Spring: March and April

Early summer: May through July

Late summer: August and September

Fall: October and November

Biennial Season: October through May

Now let's explore the challenges and changes within each of these seasons, starting with winter, the season when new seed catalogs arrive and new gardening dreams begin to take shape.

WINTER:
DECEMBER THROUGH FEBRUARY

Winter is a very real growing season in tropical areas where frost is seldom seen, but in most warm climates, it is a season for taking stock of soil and seeds and making plans for the gardening year ahead. Throughout December and January, new seed catalogs will arrive in the mail and new ideas will take root in every gardener's mind. This is the time to nourish those ideas and sort out the details that turn garden dreams into reality.

Sitting in a cozy chair on a drizzly day, thumbing through books and catalogs, you can't help but get carried away with all the possibilities up for grabs. For guaranteed satisfaction, make your selections with the following three Rational Rules for Perfect Planning in mind:

* **Grow what you like to eat, what you like to see, and what you like to smell.** Don't worry about what others think. It's none of their business.

* **Small is beautiful.** If you grow only what you love, in plots small enough to give proper care to all, you will be a happy gardener.

* **Variety is the spice of gardening life.** Always save a little space for something new and different, just to see what it will do.

The hardest part of garden planning is deciding what will go where. Sun, shade, and soil are always primary considerations, but there's also the question of how potential plant neighbors will get along with one another. Although I am a believer in companion planting, I can do it only moderately well in my own garden and will not presume to tell you how to do it in yours.

Companion planting is a subtle thing. Plants don't shout at each other, cheer each other on, or otherwise make direct, quantifiable contributions to one another's health and well-being in a way that we humans understand. Yet some plants (such as tansy) host large numbers of beneficial insects. Others (such as corn) produce excessive amounts of pollen, which attracts an extra quota of bees. Still others (such as marigolds) refuse to be parasitized by many pests, and some (such as sunflowers) furnish just the right amount of shade for their neighbors in the middle of summer.

All these plants make good companions, but they are only the beginning, for companionship is a relationship, not a thing. Companionship is the way plants share space above and below the ground, as well as how they affect the comings and goings of various insects. In cool climates, where gardens are planted more or less at one time and the gardener deals with only one group of plants in a growing season, companion planting might be a lot of fun. But in warm climates, where plantings are in a continuous state of turnover, relationships between plants become blurred.

One fact that always remains clear is that cool-natured plants grow in cool weather, while warm-natured ones like it hot. To keep turnovers simple, group like plants together. Lettuce and peas, tomatoes and peppers, and groups of fall brassicas make good plant associations. When planning rotations, perhaps you can flip-flop these groups back and forth, with legumes or cover crops wedged in between. In warm-climate gardens, companion planting has as much to do with the succession of crops as with which ones are standing side by side at any given time.

CARING FOR OVERWINTERED PLANTS

Gardeners in colder climates begin the year with bare ground, but warm-climate gardens are full of good things to eat at winter's end. All of the brassicas planted in fall are ready and should be watched closely, for they would like nothing better than to bolt into flowers. If you get lucky and the unopened flower buds of broccoli, collards, or kale go undiscovered by aphids, pluck them and eat them lightly steamed with butter. This vegetable is called broccolini. If aphids are present, you can try getting rid of them with a soap spray or by thoroughly washing the harvested buds in cold salt water, but it's quite a chore. In fact, you might let the aphids go ahead and colonize the large, topmost flower bud (their favorite), and harvest the lower side shoots for yourself.

Other hardy annuals and biennials must be picked heavily in late winter, for they will soon bolt. Dry large bunches of parsley and remove all but two or three plants. If you leave these in place for another three months, they will probably reseed. Your winter spinach also will bolt in spring, but don't waste garden time and space waiting for it to reseed, for it won't.

Even in warm climates, many plants become dormant in winter, and those described as half-hardy require winter protection to keep the roots from freezing and thawing over and over again until they become a ragged mess. Mulch to the rescue! Just watch that you don't overdo it by smothering the crowns, or central growing points, of the plants. If you cover the crowns, the plants may rot their hearts out.

PLANTING PERENNIALS

In late winter, many perennials are in the process of breaking out of a state of deep winter dormancy. It's a good time for setting out cold-hardy container-grown plants, root divisions from robust clumps already growing in your yard, and all types of dormant fruits and trees.

Controversy rages as to whether it is better to purchase container-grown or bare-rooted plants, and each side has a good case. With container-grown plants, you get more roots and they are less disturbed in transplanting. Plants whose roots are described as fibrous or brittle are best purchased in containers. These include many perennial flowers, ornamental grasses, and expensive ornamental trees.

With bare-rooted plants, both plant inspectors and you, the customer, get to examine the roots closely. Bare-rooted plants also are easier to ship, and there is little danger of importing a soil-borne pathogen. Yet bare-rooted plants need special care. Plant them immediately. The roots must never be allowed to dry out, nor should they be soaked in water for more than an hour or so. If you can't plant right away, heel them in by planting them in loose soil and heaping compost and soil over the entire root system. Buy bare-rooted plants only while they are dormant. *Before* they bud out, they need to be installed where they can stretch their roots and grow new ones. Roots can't act as water and nutrient pumps for stems and leaves if they are not firmly in contact with the soil.

(A)

(B)

Heel in plants by (A) placing them in a shallow trench and (B) heaping soil and compost over their roots.

WINTER DIRECT SEEDING

When planting seeds in winter, prepare for what heavy spring rains will do to your beautiful seedbeds. Don't forget how forceful rain can be. Just stand outside in a heavy rain, and soon your shoulders will tingle, then sting, from being hit with high-impact raindrops. In a garden, monsoon rains can turn the lightest, fluffiest seedbed into a crusted lump of mud. There are two ways to lessen this type of damage.

WINTER IN THE TROPICS
In addition to the suggestions in the Activity List for Winter below, check the Activity List for Spring (beginning on page 38) if you live in a frost-free area. Manage your space and time wisely; this is your only chance to grow cool-natured crops, but you can grow tomatoes and peppers in the spring or fall.

First, plant high in winter, in slightly raised beds or rows, with rain-induced compaction in mind. Cultivate the soil to incorporate air, and then work in some compost or other soil conditioners. When you rake over the seedbed for the last time, add a scant layer of some spongy type of organic material, such as peat moss, leaf mold, or rotted sawdust, to prevent soil crusting. Plant the seeds (not too shallow) and barely firm them in by patting them lightly with your hand or the back of a rake.

Second, sprinkle on a very light, almost see-through layer of grass clippings, almost-rotted leaves, or a bagged humus product made from composted bark. This organic matter placed right at the surface gives extra protection from crusting and compaction.

From the beginning, plan for where you will stand while weeding, thinning, or reseeding the area. Not only is it unpleasant to stand in mud, but it's bad for your soil, since it causes severe, long-term soil compaction. To distribute your weight and reduce footfall compaction, lay boards between beds or rows to use as stepping-stones, or mulch over pathways with wood chips. And, just because you've made a place to stand does not mean you need to stand there. Stay out of the garden as much as you can during rainy weather in late winter. View your accomplishments from the garden's edge.

ACTIVITY LIST FOR WINTER

SOIL

* Collect leaves and pine straw for composting and mulching. Store wood ashes collected from a fireplace or wood stove in a dry place (a metal garbage can works well). Use these materials as needed as quick-release fertilizers in acidic soil where potash is needed.

* Sow cover crops in vacant garden space. Instead of cover-cropping places scheduled to be replanted soon, mulch them over.

* Spread and incorporate mineral soil builders such as lime (in acidic soil), rock phosphate (in tight clay), greensand (where trace minerals are lacking), granite dust (for potassium), or soil sulfur (where very alkaline soil prevails).

* Chop and turn a leaf-based compost heap at least twice during the winter months to get it ready to use by spring.

* Spread and incorporate manure into garden soil that won't be planted for at least a month.

* Begin large landscaping projects.

VEGETABLES

* Ruthlessly harvest leafy greens, eat them at every opportunity, and freeze the excess. If you leave only four leaves on a spinach or turnip plant and then water it well, new leaves will quickly appear. Wait until a frost or two have come and gone before eating your collards and kale. Frost also improves the flavor of spinach.

* Where winters are severe, cover lettuce with a cold frame to keep it looking good through hard freezes.

* Plant all winter-hardy cool-weather crops, including collards, kale, parsley, leeks, parsnips, and scallions. In Zone 9, grow broccoli, beets, cauliflower, carrots, and other half-hardy cool-season crops during the winter.

* Inventory your seed collection and order new selections.

* Build or repair trellises used for summer vines.

FLOWERS

* After the blooms fade, take cuttings from tropical flowers such as bougainvillea and set them to root.

* Plant spring-flowering bulbs such as daffodils and tulips after chilling them in the refrigerator for a few weeks. If you know you have crowded clumps of daffodils but don't know exactly where they are, wait until you see the first green leaf tips emerging from the ground, then dig and divide them. If you do the job gently, the largest bulbs will still bloom.

* Plant sweet peas where you want them to grow after presoaking the seeds overnight.

* Indoors, start pansies and other cool-season annuals from seeds.

* In semitropical and tropical areas, plant Christmas poinsettias outdoors after first allowing them to dry out and become dormant in their containers.

* Move hardy annuals and perennials to where you want them to bloom in early spring. Cover them with milk-jug cloches (see page 38) after transplanting if the weather is very cold or windy.

* Weed and mulch around perennial flowers that are being left in place.

* Prune crape myrtle to shape it. New wood bears flowers.

* Plant semitropical bulbs such as crinums, alstroemerias, calla lilies, and freesias.

FRUITS

* Apply horticultural oil spray (see page 173) to fruit trees and landscape shrubs.

* If a freeze damages plants that should not be frozen, such as bananas or allamanda vines, wait until spring to give up hope. Don't prune woody tropicals too soon, as the extent of freeze damage will be easier to spot when winter is over.

* Plan additions to your fruit collection and dig planting holes in advance. Order early from regional nurseries if you want to receive dormant plants before winter's end. Because of frozen soil and frigid shipping conditions, many northern nurseries cannot begin shipping stock until March.

* Replace mulches beneath all fruit bushes and trees.

* Check wrappings on fruit tree trunks and replace them as needed.

* In late winter, prune all fruit trees and bushes.

* After pruning, fertilize fruit bushes and trees by top-dressing with composted manure, cottonseed meal, or another slow-release organic fertilizer.

Spring: March and April

Whoever said that March comes in like a lion and goes out like a lamb had the right idea, but he or she forgot a few animals and may have gotten the month wrong, too. In Zone 8, the most exciting month weatherwise may be February, or mid-February to mid-March, while Zone 7 gardeners see all of March as the chameleon month.

Whatever the calendar says, from your garden's point of view, early spring often begins like a herd of elephants. Heavy rains soak and compact the soil, while the sky stays gray for days on end. Next thing you know, morning breaks like a dove, complete with warm sunshine and a balmy breeze. The weather may then turn wild again, with the wind howling like a banshee and temperatures swinging up and down like a monkey. Just when you thought you were finished with frost, a hard one clamps down like a boa constrictor. But gardeners are optimists, and we're willing to use all types of tricks to bring out the little bit of lamb that hides within every early spring day.

We have to. If you want to have sweet lettuce, broccoli, or homegrown potatoes; to fill flower beds with flashes of calendulas and snapdragons; or to experience the satisfaction of growing perennials from seeds, you have to put early spring to good use. These and many other plants require predominantly cool weather if they are to grow well. If you wait too long to plant them, they won't be up to snuff.

A few hot days are not a problem as long as the soil temperature stays reasonably low (below 60°F). Many plants can even stand a little extra heat aboveground, as may be provided by milk carton cloches or cold frames. But in warm climates, the classic approaches to spring plant protection — such as starting plants early indoors or using cold frames — must be carefully tailored to suit the real world of the garden.

GETTING AN EARLY START

The main reason to start seeds indoors is to ensure a prompt, strong beginning for plants that need every second of mild weather that spring has to offer. If you were to go ahead and sow many seeds outdoors, they might start germinating, then stop, get rained on, and rot. To play it safe, clear off a tabletop near a south or west window, set up a fluorescent light, and start studding small containers with seeds.

Almost any seed will sprout in such a setup, but some are not worth the trouble. Take lettuce, for example. As seedlings, lettuce plants require very intense light. Even when grown within 2 inches of a grow light, they tend to be spindly. Lettuce, beets, beans, and many other vegetables are much more robust and healthy when they are direct-seeded.

In early spring, the space beneath my grow light is usually filled with flowers. Every year I experiment with something different, but I always make a point of trying some new perennial. Even perennials adapted to warm climates must enjoy a long, mild spring if they are to grow strong enough to survive the rigors of their first summer. Last year I played with butterfly bush *(Buddleia davidii)* and keys of heaven *(Centranthus rubra)*. This year it's balloon flower *(Platycodon grandiflorum)* and maiden pinks *(Dianthus deltoides)*. A grow light, put to work in early spring, invites all kinds of fascinating adventures with little-known plants and serves as a nice warm-up for the serious business of growing tomato and pepper seedlings a few weeks later, when spring really gets under way.

Let's say you've managed to grow an impressive collection of seedlings on your windowsill but you've run out of space just when it's time to get started with long-season annuals such as tomatoes, eggplant, and all sorts of warm-weather flowers. Now you need a cold frame, where the early seedlings can gradually become accustomed to the outdoors. If you harden them off in a frame, they'll be ready for their permanent homes when the last frost rolls around. For this you need a protected nursery environment — a cold frame.

If you wish, you can use a frame like the ones made for cooler climates, with tops made of glass or plastic. But you'll need an expensive model equipped with an automatic thermostat, or you'll have to stay home all the time so you can constantly open and shut the frame. In warm climates, the cold frame season is punctuated by extremely warm days. If you forget to take off a glass or plastic top, the plants beneath can burn up in a matter of hours.

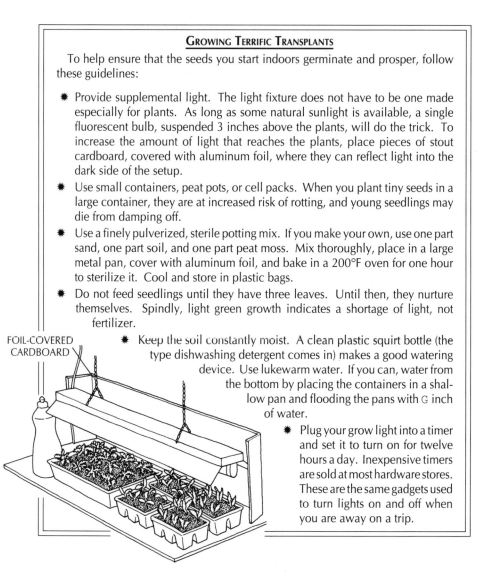

GROWING TERRIFIC TRANSPLANTS

To help ensure that the seeds you start indoors germinate and prosper, follow these guidelines:

* Provide supplemental light. The light fixture does not have to be one made especially for plants. As long as some natural sunlight is available, a single fluorescent bulb, suspended 3 inches above the plants, will do the trick. To increase the amount of light that reaches the plants, place pieces of stout cardboard, covered with aluminum foil, where they can reflect light into the dark side of the setup.

* Use small containers, peat pots, or cell packs. When you plant tiny seeds in a large container, they are at increased risk of rotting, and young seedlings may die from damping off.

* Use a finely pulverized, sterile potting mix. If you make your own, use one part sand, one part soil, and one part peat moss. Mix thoroughly, place in a large metal pan, cover with aluminum foil, and bake in a 200°F oven for one hour to sterilize it. Cool and store in plastic bags.

* Do not feed seedlings until they have three leaves. Until then, they nurture themselves. Spindly, light green growth indicates a shortage of light, not fertilizer.

FOIL-COVERED
CARDBOARD

* Keep the soil constantly moist. A clean plastic squirt bottle (the type dishwashing detergent comes in) makes a good watering device. Use lukewarm water. If you can, water from the bottom by placing the containers in a shallow pan and flooding the pans with G inch of water.

* Plug your grow light into a timer and set it to turn on for twelve hours a day. Inexpensive timers are sold at most hardware stores. These are the same gadgets used to turn lights on and off when you are away on a trip.

In warm climates, a topless frame may be better than an airtight, insulated one. The frame itself offers some wind protection, and you can cover it with a sheet of plastic or an old bedspread on frosty nights. If you can sew (or even if you can't), you can make a top for your frame out of lightweight muslin or fabric row cover (like Reemay). A fabric top allows free ventilation but buffers the wind and provides a few degrees of extra warmth. Rain can pass through it, but bugs can't. Don't depend on the fabric top for frost protection. When frost is expected, cover the frame with an old blanket to make sure the plants beneath are insulated from the cold.

A fine way to help plants make a seamless transition to life in open ground is to set them out under milk-jug cloches (see page 38). After two weeks in a cold frame, plants may be willing to make the move uncloched, but it's best to be ready to provide protection from cold snaps and stem-twisting winds after plants are set in the ground. Amass a garbage bag full of cloches. With cold-tolerant plants that are customarily set out in late winter, such as cabbage and pansies, milk jug cloches can double their growth during their first few weeks of outdoor exposure.

When working with cool-natured plants in spring, the main thing to remember is that you are gardening against the clock. The season has an indefinite beginning, with some things planted

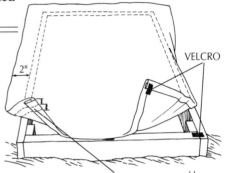

VELCRO

1" DOUBLE-THICK HEM

A Cold Frame That Breathes

After trying half a dozen homemade cold frames, here's how I made the one that I like best. If you don't sew, simply spread a double layer of row cover over your cold frame and secure the edges with boards and bricks.

1. Using scraps of ½-inch thick plywood or pine boards, build a rectangular cold frame about 4 feet wide and 3 feet deep. (This size is light enough to pick up and move around.) No side should be higher than 1 foot, or it will cast too much shade. The top may be angled or flat. Stabilize the inside corners with blocks of wood nailed into place.

2. Measure the outside dimensions of the finished frame. Cut a piece of fabric row cover or white or beige muslin into a rectangle 2 inches larger than the frame on each side. Fold under a 1-inch hem on each edge and press it in place with an iron. Set the iron on low when pressing row cover. Fold and press it again to make a 1-inch wide double-thick hem. Check to make sure the top fits the frame. Sew the hem in place using dark-colored thread.

3. Cut an 8-inch long strip of Velcro (available at fabric stores) into 1-inch pieces. (Or buy eight precut Velcro fasteners.) Separate the spiked sides of the Velcro from the fuzzy sides. At each corner of the fabric top and at midpoints on each side, sew the sharp-sided pieces of Velcro in place. Use small stitches along each edge to sew them on securely.

4. Take the top outside, match the edges to the edges of the frame, and mark where the remaining pieces of Velcro (the fuzzy pieces) should go. Staple them in place with a staple gun.

5. The frame is now ready to use. In the summer, you can make a similar fabric top out of polyester window screening or a remnant of lace, which will transform the frame into a shade house for nurturing seedlings to be set out in the fall.

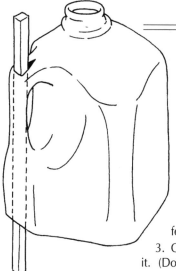

Custom-crafted milk-jug cloches are all you need to protect plants from wind, frost, and cut-worms. Here's how to cut and install them.

1. Clean empty plastic milk jugs (gallons or half gallons) with hot soapy water. Set aside the tops.
2. Place a jug upright on a sturdy surface. Using a strong knife with a sharp tip, make a V-shaped cut in the top of each handle, just above the outside curve. The cut must be big enough to accommodate a long stick, which you will poke through the handle and push into the soil below. Without this feature, milk-jug cloches disappear with the wind.
3. Cut off the bottom 2 to 3 inches of the jug and discard it. (Don't forget to recycle.) The edge does not have to be perfectly smooth and even.
4. When you set out transplants, set a milk-jug cloche over them and push 1 inch into the soil. Poke a stick through the handle and 6 inches or more into the soil below. Pile a little loose soil and mulch around the outside of the cloche. If a hard freeze comes and the plants beneath the cloches are not frost hardy, screw the tops on the milk jugs until the cold spell passes. Otherwise, leave the tops off to promote good ventilation.
5. Since milk-jug cloches do heat up inside and they limit the amount of rainfall that reaches the plants, cloched plants may need extra watering. Remove the cloches when the plants begin to grow rapidly.

while frost still lingers and others after it's gone, but it has a very definite end. In warm climates, three consecutive days of temperatures above 90°F and warm nights send an irresistible signal to many plants, telling them to change their ways and get on with reproduction. Lettuce turns bitter, spinach bolts, and cauliflower goes ricey overnight. Before the season is done, you will be turning these endings into new beginnings by planting things that are happy to see summer coming.

ACTIVITY LIST FOR SPRING

VEGETABLES AND HERBS

* Outdoors, begin direct-seeding carrots, beets, spinach, lettuce, peas, radishes, and parsley a few weeks before the last frost.
* Plant onion sets or plants. Seed scallions. Thoroughly weed

onions planted in fall and mulch them lightly to prevent soil crusting.

* Set broccoli, cauliflower, and cabbage seedlings outdoors to harden them off on sunny days for one to two weeks before setting them out. Cover them with cloches immediately after transplanting and keep the cloches on until the last frost has passed.

* Keep seed potatoes indoors, in a sunny place, until they start to sprout. Plant them on the early side of your last frost date and wait to start mulching until the plants have emerged and started to grow.

* Turn under winter cover crops or mulches. Work in plenty of manure and compost in spots where the soil needs improvement.

* Indoors, start tomatoes, peppers, and eggplant from seed. Start a second group of tomatoes a month after the first planting.

* Turn the compost heap you started last fall. Add some manure, water, and rock fertilizers (lime or rock phosphate) to get it into ready-to-use condition. Use no lime if your soil is alkaline.

* Two weeks after the last frost, begin direct-seeding these warm-weather crops: bush beans, cucumbers, dill, squash, Swiss chard, and early corn.

* In tropical and semitropical areas, plant chayote, ginger, jicama, cucuzzi gourds, and tomatillos.

FLOWERS

* Set out pansies and other hardy annuals, as well as hardy perennials started in fall and kept in containers all winter.

* Direct-seed cleome, larkspur, and other flowers that grow best in cool weather.

* Start seeds of warm-weather annuals indoors, especially those that are difficult to direct-seed, such as petunias, snapdragons, salvia, strawflowers, and vinca.

* Plant lilies around the date of your last frost.

* Plant ornamental shrubs, trees, and purchased perennials. If the plants have already begun to leaf out, provide extra water after planting.

* Fertilize daffodils and other spring-flowering bulbs with compost that has been enriched with bonemeal.

* Dig, divide, and replant chrysanthemums left in the ground from last fall.

FRUITS

* Weed, thin, and fertilize strawberries before they start to bloom. Renew the mulch if necessary.

* Plant dormant grapes, blackberries, raspberries, and blueberries.

* Plant dormant fruit trees. Wrap the trunks with hardware cloth or burlap strips to protect them from sunscald, and stake them if needed to hold them steady in the wind until new roots develop.

* Plant citrus trees wherever they are hardy.

* As soon as they leaf out, and again when they blossom, spray fruit trees and bushes with a kelp-based spray to encourage successful flowering.

EARLY SUMMER: MAY THROUGH JULY

Mulch . . . water . . . pest patrol . . . pick! This is the essential rhythm of the season, the dance that all warm-climate gardeners must do once summer boogies onto the stage. Let's discuss those essential steps in more detail.

Mulch like crazy. At first the soil will eat it up as fast as you can put it down, but after a while you won't notice your soil's insatiable consumption of mulch because your plants will be so big that you won't be able to see the ground anymore. Besides keeping moisture in the soil, a mulch serves as a barrier to soil-borne disease organisms that may venture onto your plants' leaves. Use whatever you can get your hands on — grass clippings, straw, rotted leaves, or yesterday's bush beans — and pile it on thick.

LEAKY BUCKETS

If you need to water widely spaced specimen plants or young trees, try dripping them water through plastic milk jugs or leaky plastic pails with a few holes punched in the bottom.

Water. It's precious stuff, and you really don't have the right to waste it. Besides, watering is time-consuming and not that much fun. There are several ways to water smart.

At the top of the list is drip irrigation, in which water seeps slowly into parched soil. A drip irrigation system does not have to be fancy, and many kits are quite reasonably priced. If you have a length of damaged hose around, you can make a drip line by poking holes in the hose with an ice pick and clamping off the dead end. Almost all types of drip line will last longer if you place it between soil and mulch, where the sun cannot degrade the plastic.

Drip irrigation or soaker hose systems deliver water efficiently.

Sprinklers also are nice, but unlike drip lines, they give water to weeds and walkways as well as to garden plants. In humid areas, they may aggravate various leaf spots, mildews, and slugs, since they keep leaves wet. If you plan to use a sprinkler routinely, pay close attention to timing. Ideally, you might water from five to seven in the morning.

When is the best time to water? The answer is "whenever you can." But if you live in the Southeast, where high humidity prevails, try to water in the morning. In the arid West, evening watering can increase the humidity around your plants during the nighttime hours, which often improves pollination. East or West, never water in the heat of midday or spray anything wet on plant leaves while a hot sun is shining. The aftereffects can be as devastating as throwing boiling water on your plants.

Whether you use a drip system or sprinkler or you water by hand, install a Y-type splitter at the faucet so you can have a water line dedicated to the garden. With a splitter, you will also be able to wash your hands or a bucket of squash without unscrewing the hose or dragging it across the yard.

Patrol for pests. Chapter 7 provides many details about this, but plan to spend some time picking bugs and blighted leaves at this

Y-type faucet attachment

time of year. Almost all insects are active by now, and although their numbers will increase as the summer goes on, now is when they can do the most damage. Later in the summer, there will not be nearly as much garden at risk, since you'll be growing fewer plants.

Pick. Prompt picking of ripe produce and beautiful blossoms reduces heat stress on plants and encourages them to set more flowers and fruits. Under dry conditions, plants use the nighttime hours to refill their cells with water, so you will always get the most robust specimens by picking early in the morning. Strip plants of blemished fruits or lopsided flowers as soon as you see them to keep plants from wasting energy trying to nurture them to maturity.

THE HORRORS OF HEAT-CHECK

Hot weather causes many plants to have their own little energy crises. This happens with gardeners, too. One summer when I tried to call some vegetable farmers in Florida, their answering machine said, "It's too hot to farm, so we're down at the creek." Smart strategy. In the garden, many plants also take long siestas in midsummer. They live, but they stop flowering, new growth slows to a crawl, and nothing else happens. Then fall comes, and they seem to come back to life. Tomatoes start setting fruits again, marigolds bloom anew, and many other plants that you thought were almost dead make strong comebacks.

At the heart of most heat-check problems are failed attempts at pollination. The plants in question may develop flowers, but when they are not fertilized, they shrivel up and die rather than produce fruits. The culprits are warm temperatures (above 75°F at night and above 90°F during the day), combined with very high or very low humidity. Warmth may cause the flowers and pollen grains to develop improperly, and from there they may rot, dry out, or perform the pollination process so clumsily that fertilization does not occur. This is no disaster as long as you understand what's happening.

Occasionally, you may find yourself with a garden full of exceptions to the heat-check rule. For example, a fine Gulf Coast gardener I know was kicking himself for not getting his "late" planting of 'Celebrity' tomatoes out by the first of May. As he suspected, the plants did not reach full flower until mid-June, after nights had warmed into the 70s. Under normal conditions, production would be poor, but a freak three-day cool spell in June saved the crop. The gardener did have to put shade cloth over the tomatoes for two weeks in July to protect the fruits from sunscald, but he wasn't complaining.

The best way to deal with heat-check is to expect and appreciate it. Peppers heat-check because they like to; in their native tropical home, they are perennial. Instead of getting frustrated with them in midsummer, think about all those nice peppers you'll be eating in the fall. Don't pull out marigolds that stop flowering if the plants look healthy. Instead, start watering them when nights cool down in early fall and look forward to a heavy flush of fall flowers. With indeterminate tomatoes, prune off all injured parts in early summer to conserve water and induce branching. If the plants are still living in late summer, fertilize and water them to promote new growth.

Sometimes hot weather will cause wholesale crop failure for bush beans due to failed flowering and subsequent fruit set. If this happens, turn the plants under as a cover crop or pull them up and use them as mulch. A few varieties of bush beans, including 'Provider', will try to blossom again. Half-runners and pole beans have a better chance of escaping heat-check, since they always blossom again and again.

SUMMER PLANTING

Despite the heat, summer is not a lost time for planting. You can start more seeds indoors, provided the species you choose really like hot weather. Basil, gomphrena, and marigolds are a nice trio to start with. Let all late seedlings develop a hefty root system before you set them out to cook in the hot sun. (I grow them in half-shade until the roots fill 2-inch pots.) Transplant them late in the day, during a period of cloudy weather, and water them for at least a week. Temporary shade covers, such as pots or boxes popped over new transplants, can dramatically improve survival rates.

Summer is an excellent time to propagate houseplants, whether you are air layering a schefflera or dividing up aloe plantlets. Bear in mind that propagation is quite different from repotting. Save routine repotting of houseplants until late summer, for there is little to be gained by doing it now. In cases where plants will need to grow new root systems by winter, go ahead and propagate.

SUMMER COVERS

The part of summer when nothing much will grow is fast approaching, and chances are that your garden is showing a few bare patches where spring crops have come and gone. Cover-crop them! Buckwheat and soybeans are good choices in all warm climates, and crowder peas work well, too. Buckwheat can be allowed to stand until it flowers, but turn under soybeans or crowder peas when the first blossoms appear. Once reproduction commences, these plants start using up the nitrogen they have fixed and stored in their roots.

ACTIVITY LIST FOR EARLY SUMMER

VEGETABLES AND HERBS

* Provide water as needed for cool-weather crops that have lingered into summer. Harvest them promptly, for they won't last long in the hot weather. Keep potatoes very well mulched to protect them from the sun; dig them in the evening on a cloudy day.

* Set out more tomatoes, peppers, and eggplant. Plant sweet potato slips. Stake or cage early tomatoes.

* Direct-seed the following vegetables in prepared beds or rows: bush beans, pole beans, asparagus beans, lima beans, corn, cucumbers, cantaloupe, okra, watermelon, squash, Malabar spinach, peanuts, and gourds. Wait until the hot weather

arrives to fill out the vegetable garden with southern peas such as crowders and black-eyed peas.

* Direct-seed dill where you want it to grow. Basil is best started indoors and transplanted. Sow a second crop of both these versatile herbs when the first planting starts to flower.

FLOWERS

* Continue planting hot-natured annuals such as celosia, impatiens, marigolds, gomphrena, melampodiums, portulacas, vincas, sunflowers, and zinnias. Pinch back chrysanthemums to make them bushy.

* Plant dahlias, gladiolus, caladiums, and other semitropical bulbs.

* Now that the soil is warm and south-facing walls heat up during the day, try screening them with fast-growing annual vines such as hyacinth bean vines *(Dolichos lablab)*, black-eyed Susan vines *(Thunbergia)*, and morning glories.

* If they need shaping, prune azaleas, forsythias, and other shrubs that bloomed in spring.

* Cut back bougainvillea vines that are too big to manage.

FRUITS

* Thin tree fruits so that the green fruits are at least 4 inches apart.

* Fertilize berries and begin irrigating them. Mow regularly around all fruit bushes and trees to discourage insects. Enjoy your berry harvest.

* Mulch strawberries heavily to help retain soil moisture.

LATE SUMMER: AUGUST AND SEPTEMBER

For me, the most difficult time of year is August, when the soil dries into deep cracks, everything seems to wilt no matter how much I water, and cool evenings — prime time for pulling up dead plants and readying their replacements — are few and far between. Just providing moisture for plants that really need it seems to take up every spare minute, while passing clouds tease me daily into thinking a thunderstorm will finally come. So, I take a short break (really the only alternative when it's at least 95°F every day) and devote my limited gardening energy to keeping herbs, peppers, azaleas, dogwoods, berries, and assorted other beloved plants alive.

While we gardeners are slogging along, struggling to keep our blood simmering at a mere 98.6°F, storm systems in the tropics are boiling to life. As they push themselves northward toward land, first as tropical waves and later as hurricanes, both we and our plants are in for some excitement. In the West, they call them monsoons, the wettest rains of the year. In the East, the sauna syndrome kicks in: hot, humid mornings, towering clouds in early afternoon, a drenching rain, and then just enough sun to saturate the air for another humid night.

Timing is challenging at all times of the year, but late-summer gardening is especially tricky because the days are getting shorter instead of longer, and this causes plants to slow down. On average, you can add three weeks to a crop's estimated days to maturity when you grow it in late summer and fall. If you want to make the most of all possibilities, you will also be working with both warm-season and cool-season plants. To make everything work out right, you must get involved in strategic planning.

SCHEDULING LATE-SUMMER PLANTING

First, try to pinpoint your first frost date. Ninety days before that is when you need to finish up planting of all warm-season crops. If you start at least three months before the first frost date, you can often grow bountiful fall crops of squash, cucumbers, beans, okra, basil, marigolds, petunias, and celosia.

Once you hit the ninety-day mark, it's time to think about things that take a while to get started and need to mature in cool weather: broccoli, cauliflower, Chinese cabbage, spinach, fennel, pansies, nasturtiums, and calendulas. In Zone 7, this change from planting warm-season crops to planting cool-season crops occurs in August. In Zone 9, it happens at the end of September.

Regardless of which group of plants you are working with, the challenges of starting plants under hot conditions are the same. For reasons unknown, I do not get good results starting seeds indoors in late summer; it's almost as though they know there's a better world waiting on the other side of the window. Sometimes I keep them on a windowsill until the seeds germinate and then put them in a shady place outdoors.

Just as in spring, the activities of late summer require that you have a quantity of some type of potting mix on hand. I have good luck mixing up my own, using the compost that has emerged from a summer's worth of gardening. I use one part river sand, one part compost, and one part bagged potting soil, mixed well. If some hot days are in the offing, I leave the mix in my black wheelbarrow, dampen it, cover it with clear plastic, and let it sit a couple of days. Under the plastic, the mixture heats up quite a bit, and I'm sure some seeds, weeds, and misplaced earth critters are killed in the process.

SHADE DEVICES

All young plants that have been started indoors and those that have

PAPER-TOWEL PRESPROUTING

When the weather is hot and dry, many seeds have trouble sprouting, since they can't stay saturated with water for the time required for germination. To help them along, presprout them indoors within the folds of damp paper towels. Thoroughly dampen a paper towel and sprinkle on the seeds (bean, carrot, cucumber, or whatever). Fold the paper towel into thirds and place it inside a plastic bag. Most seeds will germinate and be ready to plant in two days. Presprouted seeds survive best if they are planted as soon as the seed coat splits open and the sprout begins to show. When planting presprouted seeds, keep them constantly moist for five days after planting.

been growing in containers in the shade will need to be shaded for the first week or two after they are set out in the garden. This goes for late tomatoes, annual flowers, and cool-season vegetables such as fall broccoli and cauliflower, which often must be planted while summer still rages if they are to mature before hard freezes become frequent.

Several things work well. Cardboard boxes, with their bottoms removed, can be placed around transplants. I leave a flap attached at each end and place bricks on the flaps to hold the boxes in place. Or, you can place a wooden pallet, held high by several bricks or concrete blocks, over the plants. If you want your garden to look professional, install a series of plastic pipe hoops over the row and cover it with shade cloth or light-colored muslin (see pages 20-21). Where only a few plants are involved, it's simplest to cover them with clay flowerpots for a few days after transplanting.

REDUCING WATERING CHORES

The smart watering using drip irrigation recommended for early summer (see page 41) is the best way to water plants in late summer, too. But frugal watering will not protect all plants from the ravages of late summer's heat. Sometimes it's best to let plants cope with the season in their own ways rather than provide water every time they want a drink. Drought is a reality of late-summer gardening in hot climates, but there are ways to avoid spending every spare minute doling out precious water to plants.

> ### Sunflower Screens
> Virtually no plant wants full sun this time of year. A row of sunflowers, planted along the south or west side of direct-seeded parsley, bush beans, or cucumbers, can provide just enough shade to keep the adjoining bed from drying out. The sunflowers mature quickly and can be pulled out when fall gets under way and the cool-season crops can handle more sun. Intermediate-height sunflowers work best. Corn and okra also make good sunscreens.

* Water container-grown plants as often as they need it. If plants wilt every day and appear potbound, repotting to larger containers will make them healthier and easier to water. Still, you may need to water them every day.

* Don't water lawns until after they become semidormant from heat stress. Don't mow them either. In times of drought, grasses concentrate available moisture in their crowns, and that's the only part of the plants you really need to keep alive.

* Water young trees and newly planted nursery stock, but don't use your hose. Deep drip watering is better. Punch a single small hole in the bottom of a gallon plastic milk jug, fill the jug with water, and place it under the shrub or tree (you may need several). This spot-drip method is efficient in terms of both time and water usage, and it gets the water deep into the soil, where the plants can make the best use of it.

* If your vegetables or fruits dry out completely, restore soil moisture gradually rather than soaking the soil all at once. Tomatoes, grapes, melons, and many other fruit-bearing plants will split or crack when given a big drink after a dry spell.

* Use available shade, replenish mulches after watering, and pick often.

ACTIVITY LIST FOR LATE SUMMER

VEGETABLES

* Outdoors, start off this season by planting seeds of bush snap beans, Swiss chard, cucumbers, and squash. Soak seeds in water the night before you plant them and cover the seeded bed or row with a piece of cardboard, a board, or a shade pallet for three days after planting.

* Mulch heavily beneath peppers, or stake them securely. Start watering tomatoes well. Top back okra plants to encourage bushiness. Dig sweet potatoes and peanuts.

* Plant any potatoes that have begun to sprout and mulch them well.

* Indoors, plant broccoli, cauliflower, scallion, leek, and possibly cabbage, brussels sprouts, kale, and celery seeds. Use a fluorescent plant light to encourage strong growth.

* In the nursery bed, take cuttings of perennial herbs and sink them in pots of soil to root. Keep them shaded for three weeks.

* Toward the end of the season, start direct-seeding leafy greens: lettuce, spinach, mustard, Chinese cabbage, turnips, beets, collards, and kale. Use radishes as markers between different vegetables. Also plant parsley where you want it to grow through the winter.

WADING-POOL WISDOM

When the water in my child's wading pool gets too dirty for playing, I siphon it to my vegetables. This works as long as the pool is a few inches higher than my garden.

Place one end of a garden hose in the pool and the other end near a thirsty group of plants. Straighten any kinks or knots in the hose. Crouch down, pick up the end of the hose near the plants, and blow into it. Immediately take a deep breath, exhale, and then suck on the hose as hard as you can. Put the hose down. A trickle of water should appear within ten seconds. If it doesn't, repeat the procedure up to three times. Sometimes it takes a few sucks to get the hose sufficiently full of water to make the siphon action work.

You can also use a rigid wading pool as a shallow pond in which to set chronically thirsty containerized plants. Place an inch or so of water in the pool, and you can water each pot from the bottom without wetting the plant's foliage. If you will be away from home in the summer and ask a friend to water for you, this strategy will ease his or her task considerably.

---

* In vacant garden space, sow a quick cover crop of crowder peas.

FLOWERS

* Pull up tired petunias, zinnias, and marigolds. Plant marigold, nasturtium, and calendula seeds outdoors for a late blast of summer color.

* Divide and reset irises. Daylilies also may be divided if you want to turn a few clumps into a dozen. (See illustration, page 126.) Water roses and chrysanthemums to encourage lasting fall blossoms.

* Indoors, sow pansy, ornamental kale, foxglove, hollyhock, Siberian wallflower, and sweet william seeds, along with any new perennials you want to grow from seeds.

* Toward the end of this season, plant bachelor's buttons, larkspur, poppies, and Shasta daisies where you want them to bloom in the spring. Pinch leafy rosettes from coreopsis and other plants with big crowns and sink them into cultivated soil to grow roots. (See illustration, page 126.)

FRUITS

* Mow and rake beneath all fruit trees to interrupt disease cycles.
* Begin mulching beneath blueberries and bramble fruits.
* Provide plenty of water for fall-bearing raspberries.
* Water strawberries and prepare a new home for young runners. Dig and move the runners when the weather cools.

FALL: OCTOBER AND NOVEMBER

This is the season when nongardening visitors, trying to make conversation, will say, "I guess your garden's about gone for this year." "Oh, not yet," you may respond. "I'm still picking snap beans, squash, herbs, cucumbers, tomatoes, and peppers. As soon as it cools down a bit, I'll have you over for turnip greens."

If the truth be told, fall is the most enjoyable gardening season of the year. Bugs are tired of reproducing, the soil is able to hold on to moisture, and gorgeous blue skies and balmy breezes make outdoor work downright fun. Plus, there are plenty of good things to grow.

Granted, fall is a quickie season that can be somewhat tricky, for temperatures swing from hot to cold and back again, and the same things that grow at a frenetic pace in spring plod along like turtles in fall. But once you understand the possibilities and pinpoint a few pivotal planting dates, the fall season is packed with rewards.

Fall coincides with the first phase of the biennial season, which is discussed later in this chapter. Here I'll concentrate on gardening activities for the fast and frenzied fall season — the relatively short period that begins when nights cool down in late September and ends when hard freezes occur in late November and early December.

As long as soil temperatures remain warm, you may still plant many vegetables of a temperate nature, although they will mature much more slowly than when planted in spring. For example, bush snap beans, rated at forty-five days to maturity, often require sixty days when planted in the fall. Once they do begin setting beans, however, the beans will stay in good shape on the plants for a long time. I seeded my first trial of the 'Derby' variety on Labor Day, and I was still picking crisp beans when November rolled around. By covering the beans with an old mattress pad on frosty nights, that planting of beans continued to bear for more than a month.

Beans are just one example of the many temperate-natured vegetables you can grow in fall, but the stars of any fall garden are the leafy greens, many of which can be grown successfully only in fall. If you plant turnips, mustard, or spinach in spring, you may get a crop for a couple of weeks, then long, warm

BEETS	LETTUCE	COLLARD	TURNIP	KALE	CHINESE CABBAGE	SPINACH
Days to Maturity						
50-60	40-50	60	40-50	70	50	50-60
Frosts Needed to Enhance Flavor						
0	0	1	0	3	0	1
Cold Hardiness*						
30°	34°	18° Long Standing	28°	12° Long Standing	34°	18° Long Standing

* Varies with variety, prior weather conditions, and protection provided

days will cause the plants to turn bitter and bolt. Not so in the fall. This is *the* time to plant leafy greens with wild abandon, for they only get better as days shorten and nights become cool.

This is not to say that leafy greens are hardy enough to come through hard freezes unscathed. With few exceptions, they will not. Frost may cause the leaves to burn, so you might want to cover your lettuce and other greens with a light blanket or floating row cover when frost is likely. If you live in an area where aphids and cucumber beetles persist into the fall, floating row cover will also keep them and other bugs from marring the beauty of your delicious greens.

Fall is also the season to think Oriental. Bok choy and daikon radishes grow best in the fall, along with Chinese cabbage, mizuna (Japanese mustard), and shungiku (an edible chrysanthemum). If you start the seeds very early in the fall, Oriental herbs such as coriander (cilantro) and garlic chives will be large enough to pick by the time other Oriental vegetables are ready for the wok.

In Zones 9 and 10, the situation is different. With frost not looming in the immediate future, or possibly not at all, the time is at hand for planting vegetables that have a hard time with summer's heat: carrots, beets, peas, celery, and anything else billed as a cool-weather crop. You can even try your hand at warm-season crops such as tomatoes and peppers, although it's better to wait until late winter, when days are becoming longer instead of shorter.

In semitropical climates, this is the time to have fun with flowers northerners grow in the summer: annual alyssum, calendulas, nasturtiums, phlox, snapdragons, and sweet peas. The possibilities are endless, and it's likely that your yard will have more color in November than at any other time of year. Peruse catalogs for flowers categorized as cool-season annuals and try two or three new ones each year, bearing in mind that a tropical winter is much like summer in Vermont.

FORCED FRAGRANT BULBS

Most warm-climate gardeners are well advised to refrigerate spring-flowering bulbs such as daffodils, narcissi, and crocuses for a few weeks before planting them outdoors in early winter. You may want to force the most fragrant ones into bloom early and grow them in pots you can bring indoors. Here's how to do it:

1. Select compact, fragrant varieties such as 'Cragford' or 'Minnow' narcissi, or any hyacinths. Refrigerate the bulbs until the

soil cools down in late October or November.

2. Plant the bulbs in clay pots with the tops barely covered with gritty potting soil. Water until thoroughly dampened.

3. Outdoors, dig a narrow trench long enough to accommodate the pots. (Later in the winter, you can use this trench as a planting site for various perennials or bulbs.) Place the pots in the trench and cover them with straw or leaves.

4. After a month, check to see if fat, pale growing tips have emerged from the bulbs. When this happens, lift the pots, wash them off, and set them in full sun for a few days.

5. When the growing tips turn green, bring the pots indoors and set them in a cool, sunny location. Within three weeks, fragrant blossoms should be ready to show off.

6. After the flowers fade, move the pots to a protected place outdoors. Feed and water the plants periodically. When the foliage withers, allow the soil to dry out. Store the bulbs indoors in a cool, dry place through the summer, and then plant them outdoors the following fall.

THE SOIL IN THE FALL

In addition to growing a robust fall garden, this is the season to start strengthening your soil. Leaves are falling, and poultry houses, horse stables, and dairy barns are being cleaned out in preparation for winter. Put these resources together, and you have the makings of a fine winter compost heap.

You might want to pile your leaves separately, as they won't begin to rot until they have been thoroughly leached by rain or water from your hose. Rotted leaves are rich sources of organic matter, but fresh ones actually tie up soil nutrients and moisture. Besides, if you set leaves aside to leach, you can quickly establish an active microbial compost colony by mixing fresh manure with old mulches, dead plants, and other garden debris, lightened a bit with the last of the

A NOTE ON BAGWORMS

Pecan and hickory trees sometimes host colonies of bagworms in the fall. These webby masses are filled with tiny caterpillars. Although you might want to treat heavily infested trees with a *Bacillus thuringiensis* (Bt) insecticide to kill the worms, don't worry if a tree has only one colony. These worms seldom venture outside their nests to feed, and the leaves they do eat are going to fall in a few weeks anyway. Live and let live, and save yourself a lot of trouble.

TOWERING TOMATO CAGES

TOWERING TOMATO CAGES

Do you use cages made of concrete-reinforcing wire to grow your tomatoes? If so, turn them into towers of compost when the tomatoes don't need them anymore. Move the cages to a cultivated spot and gradually fill them with garden debris, leaves, and an occasional shovelful of manure. Dampen the material as you add it. In late winter, remove the cages and chop and blend the material well. By spring it will be ready to turn into the soil, right where it sits.

season's grass clippings. In a month or so, when the manure is half composted and there is nothing much else to do, you can spend a few hours putting the leaves and manure mixture together, creating your biggest and best compost heap of the year.

TO MULCH OR COVER-CROP?

If sections of your garden are to remain unused during the winter months, there are two ways to keep the soil "growing" during its vacation. You can either mulch it or plant it with a cover crop. Both are attractive to the eye and a real boon to your soil's health. Here are some things to think about when deciding what to do.

Will the space be needed first thing in the spring? If so, go with mulch. Prepare the soil for planting before you mulch it. That way, if the soil is terribly wet in late winter, when you want to plant peas or potatoes, you can pull back the mulch and plant without cultivating first.

Do you like to look at swaths of green and you don't mind mowing? Then by all means grow some annual rye, wheat, or cereal rye during the winter months. These hardy cover crops are a treat to the eye on dreary winter days, but you do have to mow them from time to time and till them under in early spring. If you don't have a Rototiller, you can pull up the plants, compost them, and return the material to the soil in refined form. Grassy cover crops such as wheat and rye are great for soil (such as thin sand or tight clay) that needs lots of organic matter added. As they rot, they emit chemicals that inhibit sprouting of many weed seeds.

Are you transforming a place that was planted with grass into a vegetable or flower garden? If so, you definitely need a cover crop, preferably a nitrogen-fixing legume such as clover or Austrian winter peas. The cover crop will wake up the soil, biologically speaking, and improve its texture by filling it with roots. Plus, the cultivating you'll do while growing the cover crop will disturb grubs and other sod-loving creatures, giving you a head start on cutworm problems next spring.

If you can't decide which cover crop to plant, look for fall cover crop blends in your favorite seed catalog. Try them in a small area. Chances are you will fall in love with the lush greenery. If you like a particular plant in the mixture, next year you can plant it by itself as your winter garden cover.

WHAT'S YOUR pH?

Fall is the traditional season for testing the soil's pH — a measure of acidity or alkalinity that radically affects how well plants are able to absorb nutrients present in the soil. Inexpensive pH test kits are available at garden supply stores. Use three soil samples, taken from different places in your garden, to get an accurate reading of your pH situation.

If your soil is extremely acidic, add lime to the soil, the compost heap, and the mulch pile. If it is extremely alkaline, find all the leaves you can and set them to rotting, for they are acidic by nature. Most plants can tolerate a rather broad pH range, so don't worry about the numbers too much. You don't need a pH of exactly 6.0, the rating deemed best for most plants. Check your pH at least every three years, or more often if plants frequently appear malnourished.

In addition to lime, which is used primarily to raise the pH of acidic soils, other mineral soil conditioners are best applied in the fall or winter. Rock phosphate and gypsum can help open up tight, compacted clay. Granite dust and greensand supply slow-release potash. All rock soil builders are heavy to tote but cheap to buy, and they are a long-lasting, sustainable way to keep good quotas of major and minor nutrients in your soil. You can even sprinkle them into your compost heap for a nice finishing touch.

Although I don't discuss evergreen ornamental shrubs separately in this book, it would be unfair to zip through fall without noting that this is the best time to plant them. When planted in fall, they benefit from winter rains and sun — their favorite kind. Buy container-grown or balled-and-burlapped evergreens and conifers soon after they arrive at the garden center, when they are freshly dug. Plant them in well-loosened holes, spreading the roots in the process, and water and mulch them well.

ACTIVITY LIST FOR FALL

VEGETABLES AND HERBS

* Plant cool-season vegetables, including spinach, lettuce, turnips, kale, parsley, and Oriental greens. Keep the seedbed moist to encourage fast germination. Sow scallion, leek, and

fennel seeds in flats. Keep all plants thinned to the desired spacing.

* Harvest all warm-season vegetables before the first killing frost. Tomatoes and peppers can be held through a brief spell of cold weather by covering them with old blankets until the warm weather returns.

* Dig sweet potatoes and set them to cure in a single layer in a warm, airy place. Cure peanuts and winter squash, too.

* Monitor fall greens for aphids and other pests, or keep the plants covered with floating row cover. Begin picking greens when nights become consistently cool.

* Clean up all old plants, roots and all, and chop and compost them. Cultivate vacant areas to expose buried pests to weather and birds.

* Plant cover crops where you need organic matter and improved weed control. These provide lush greenery through the winter.

* Collect leaves and other mulch materials and set them aside to weather.

* Add lime or sulfur to your soil if indicated by a pH test. Other mineral fertilizers may also be added as you clean and cultivate the soil.

FLOWERS

* Plant the seeds of hardy annuals and perennials. Cool-season annuals that can tolerate only a light frost may be planted in Zones 9 and 10.

* Purchase and prechill spring-flowering bulbs. Force some in containers. Dig and divide crowded clumps.

* Remove mulches from roses and other disease-prone plants. Replace them with fresh, clean material.

* Dig and store warm-natured bulbs such as caladiums and dahlias. It is not necessary to dig gladioli, which are usually winter hardy in warm climates.

* Plant ornamental evergreen trees and shrubs.

FRUITS

* Weed and thin strawberry plants before mulching them well with pine straw. Plant new beds with young runners taken from the old plantings.

* Mow and rake beneath all fruit bushes and trees to interrupt the life cycles of various pests. Lay down clean mulches beneath berries. Declare war on Bermuda grass and dig it out from around blueberries and other fruits before mulching the plants.

* Rewrap the trunks of young fruit trees to protect them from sunscald.

BIENNIAL SEASON: OCTOBER THROUGH MAY

The biennial season is so important in warm climates that it must be given its own space. It's the only way we can work with cool-season annuals, or with many perennials that burn out in their first summer. Gardening in the biennial season also serves as a horticultural and spiritual bridge — a way of experiencing the connections between fall, winter, and spring.

The biennial season is a cycle that matches the life spans of various plants categorized as annuals, biennials, and perennials. True biennials may be grown only during the biennial season, since they require the swing from warm, to cold, and then to cool weather that characterizes fall to winter to spring. Yet many hardy annuals also find the biennial season to their liking. Numerous perennials that are short-lived because of summer's extreme heat are best treated as biennials and replanted every fall, either from seeds or cuttings. And then there are the onions, which behave in all sorts of strange ways, reproductively speaking, depending on the weather to which they are exposed.

The biennial season is the time to experiment with the unknown, to try plants seldom seen in your area, and to have fun. It's one of the special privileges awarded gardeners lucky enough to live in warm climates.

Take sweet peas, for example, those fragrant, dainty flowers English gardeners grow as easily as we grow zinnias. If you live in Florida, you must grow them during the biennial season or not at all. Ditto calendulas, stocks, dianthus species, and countless other beautiful flowers.

The most unmanageable part of the biennial season is its beginning. It's tough to get enthusiastic about planting seeds when leaves are beginning to fall and winter is in the air. But start you must if your plants are to realize their full potential. Remember, most of the plants you'll work with are best suited to maritime climates (which never get very hot or very cold) or to places with long, cool summers. You can't waste a minute, because the party will be over in spring when hot weather sets in.

GROWING BIENNIAL PLANTS

If you're a vegetable gardener at heart and resent spending time on flowers when you could be growing tomatoes, the biennial season eases your dilemma, for there are literally hundreds of species of flowers you may play with as biennials but only a handful of vegetables.

The following list can help stir your imagination, but it's only a beginning. When ordering seeds, look for plants categorized as half-hardy perennials, cool-season annuals, or biennials. An asterisk follows plants that are not winter hardy in most of Zone 7.

Edibles

Beets*

Brussels sprouts*

Celery*

Mints

Onions, including leeks, scallions, and garlic

Parsley

Parsnips

Potatoes*

Sage

Spinach

Strawberries

Flowers

All hardy annuals, biennials, and fast-growing perennials, including:

Alyssum

Baby's-breath *(Gypsophila elegans)*

Bachelor's-button

Calendula*

Candytuft

Dianthus *(Dianthus chinensis)**

Maiden pink *(Dianthus deltoides)*

Myosotis

Nasturtium*

Pansy

Penstemon

Poppy

Shasta daisy

Snapdragon*

Statice

Stock*

Sweet pea*

Sweet William

Wallflower *(Cheiranthus cheiri and C. allionii)*

STARTING SEEDS

Most plants grown as biennials begin their lives as seeds, although those that are really short-lived perennials, such as sage and sweet William, are easily propagated from stem cuttings taken from weak plants just before you throw the rest of their ravaged bodies into the compost heap. When you're starting seeds, it's always best to use fresh seeds, especially various onions. I have found that keeping the seeds in the refrigerator for three weeks before planting often enhances germination. The seeds then think it's spring, a natural season for sprouting.

Just as in spring, it's often easiest to sow seeds in flats or cell packs indoors and keep them under lights until they germinate. You can set up your seedling nursery outdoors however, if the site is well shaded and you are able to water daily. After you plant the seeds, try covering the flats with newspaper for a few days. Remove the cover as soon as the first sprouts appear.

Fall-sown seedlings must be hardened off gradually, even when no threat of frost exists. Autumn sunshine is often intense, and seedlings started indoors must become accustomed to it very gradually. At first, set them out for only an hour or two, gradually increasing their exposure. Otherwise, tender young leaves may burn, turning pale green or even withering to brown.

When your seedlings are large enough to handle, their roots are becoming crowded, and they've been hardened off, you can transplant them outdoors or move them into larger containers. If you haven't decided exactly where you want them, go with containers, since many of the plants grown during the biennial season can be set out all winter long. In Zone 7, where winter sometimes becomes violent, you might opt for containers so you can bring your plants into the garage if an ice storm strikes. Usually it does not hurt to delay final transplanting until late winter.

Because of the waning days, plants grown during the biennial season typically start out slowly. By the time winter sets in, they will be small rosettes or miniature plants that may hardly grow at all for a month or two. Then, as soon as the days start getting longer and warm up a bit, they will burst forth with new growth.

If you plant them in the ground (the best option in Zones 8, 9, and 10), be careful that you don't mulch over the crowns. A little mulch for winter protection is a good idea, but too much mulch will promote rotting. If very cold weather threatens, cover the plants for a few days with a cardboard box (held in place with a brick or flowerpot) or a light layer of pine straw needles.

Get all your cool-natured plants in the ground by winter's end. As soon as days lengthen and the soil begins to warm, they may need a bit of food. Mulch around them with compost if you have it, or top-dress with an organic fertilizer. The idea is to provide optimal growing conditions, thus eliminating any obstacles to fast growth.

One of the most beautiful things about the biennial season is that it keeps you gardening. Your collection may be small, but at least you have something living and green to watch and admire as fall, winter, and spring flow together into one.

Chapter Three

THE GOURMET GARDEN

I CAN'T IMAGINE GOING A YEAR without a vegetable garden, mostly because I like to eat good food. Whether I'm savoring the crisp chill of early winter captured in a spinach leaf or the hot power of summer compressed into a sweet potato, eating homegrown garden produce is a supreme culinary and horticultural experience.

There is no better food than the freshest possible version, grown organically in good soil. Compared to purchased produce, homegrown vegetables are more nutritious (compliments of rich, healthy soil and shortened time in storage), they taste better (the ultimate legacy of plenty of trace nutrients in the soil), and they are more digestible. It's a delicate topic, but let's just say that when a salad's ingredients come from healthy, balanced soil, it causes no gastric distress. Maybe it has to do with the water supermarket vegetables drink, or perhaps agricultural chemicals are to blame. I really don't know. But if everybody started growing their own vegetables, manufacturers of antacids and various gas-relieving products might be in big trouble.

Another reason homegrown vegetables are superior to store-bought ones is the varieties themselves. When a commercial grower selects varieties, he or she must consider how the product will hold up to shipping once it's ready to sell. They need tomatoes with strong shoulders, bruise-resistant lettuce, and carrots tough enough to be dug with machines. The home gardener has no such worries and can grow many varieties so delicate that they will never be seen in stores. I once grew a neat Italian heirloom tomato that bruised as easily as a ripe peach. There's no telling what it would have looked like after a long ride in a truck.

Age also is a factor in the fine quality of homegrown produce. Few commercial farmers are willing to pick tiny, shiny squash when they can wait a week and let the vegetables double in size. There is simply no comparison between tender young turnip greens picked a leaf at a time and the tough, strong-flavored mature greens sold in stores. And no food scientists have figured out how to make sweet shell peas hold their sugars in storage. Either you get them fresh off the vine, or you eat starchy peas.

Enough of arguing my case. Let's get on with the particulars of growing great vegetables in warm climates. First I'll explain a few practical strategies to work into your garden plan, and then I'll review more than 60 promising vegetables and the best ways to grow them.

The first step is to sort the vegetables you want to grow into their appropriate seasons and order some seeds. Chapter 2 explores planting seasons in detail, but here is a quick break down of a few common vegetables.

Cool-Season Crops for Winter, Early Spring, or Fall

Beets	Kohlrabi
Broccoli	Leeks
Cabbage	Lettuce
Carrots	Onions
Cauliflower	Peas, garden
Chard	Potatoes
Chinese cabbage	Radishes
Collards	Salsify
Fennel	Scallions
Greens	Spinach
Kale	Turnips

Warm-Season Vegetables to Grow in Summer

Amaranth	Peas, field
Beans	Peanuts
Cantaloupes	Peppers

Corn	Pumpkins
Cucumbers	Squash
Eggplant	Sweet potatoes
Gourds	Tomatillos
Jicama	Tomatoes
Okra	Watermelons

Gardening in New Soil

Building good soil takes time, and some vegetables grow better in relatively unimproved soil than others. To ensure success your first season, rely heavily on these light feeders. In naturally acidic soil, go with beans, carrots, garlic, peppers, squash, and turnips. In naturally alkaline soil, emphasize peas, okra, leaf lettuce, and pumpkins.

Perennials and Perpetuals That Live Year-Round

Artichokes	Garlic
Asparagus	Nest and multiplying onions
Chayote	Perennial herbs

I get so excited about outstanding varieties that I can't help but drop a few names, especially those that are extra-delicious, extra–pest resistant, or unique in color or form. Your Extension Service also can provide a list of recommended varieties. But please, conduct your own trials and let your taste buds be your guide when choosing which varieties to plant. Chapter 8 lists more than twenty sources for top-quality seeds.

Once you've chosen your favorite crops, it's time to plan rotations and planting sequences. This can be a lot of fun, but only experience will teach you the best planting dates and crop rotations for your garden. The box below provides some basic ideas to get you started. From there, you're a free bird when it comes to discovering whether you can grow good crops of your favorite

Long-Season Succession Cropping

The miniclimate in your garden will support a number of unique combinations of vegetables within the same growing season. Here are some sample schemes to get you thinking.

On a Trellis

Garden peas → Cucumbers → Cowpea cover crop → Kale

Garden peas → Tomatoes → Winter cover crop

Spring cover crop → Pole beans → Cucumbers → Lettuce

In Beds or Rows

Spinach → Bush beans → Cowpeas → Leeks

Lettuce → Peppers → Garlic

Carrots → Cowpeas → Fall greens

Potatoes → Shell beans → Fall greens

vegetables back to back.

My final advice to budding vegetable gardeners is to try new things — new species, new varieties, and new ways to grow them. Just because unusual vegetables such as adzuki beans and tomatillos are not included in many gardens does not mean you can't grow them. Regional heirlooms, such as 'Red Ripper' crowder peas in the Southeast and 'Tepary' beans in the Southwest, are always strong candidates. In addition, Chinese vegetables can quickly become mainstays in a fall garden, and European mesclun mixtures may become your favorite spring greens.

I always save a corner for something weird that I've never grown before, just to see what it will do. Sometimes these experiments fail; to me, arugula tastes like old tires and superhot peppers are about as useful as sizzling sticks of dynamite. But I love orange tomatoes, miniature basil, kohlrabi, and many other vegetables that I might never have tasted had I not grown my own. To a vegetable gardener, these adventures into the unknown are natural dramas that shouldn't be missed.

SIXTY VIGOROUS VEGETABLES

AMARANTH

Varieties: Through meticulous selection over thousands of years, the weed commonly known as pigweed has been transformed into a talented and ornamental grain crop. Cultivated varieties bear huge seed heads that are harvested when dry, at the end of the season. The grains can be popped like popcorn or crushed and added to homemade breads and cooked cereals. When the plants are young, leaves can be used as a substitute for cooked spinach. A few plants, grown at the garden's edge or perhaps in the middle where they will shade other crops, have a dramatic effect.

Seasons: Plant in the spring after the last frost and keep moist until the seeds have germinated. Amaranth has very deep roots and requires scant soil fertility and minimal watering after it becomes established.

Tips:

❋ Allow plants to grow all summer, then harvest them before the seeds start to drop.

* Amaranth also may be used as a warm-weather cover crop.

ARTICHOKES

Types and varieties: Two totally unrelated plants are known as artichokes. The true artichoke is a perennial thistle in which the edible part is the large, unopened flower bud. The most widely available variety, 'Green Globe', is reputed to produce heads in its first year, but it is very unpredictable. The most dependable production does not come from seedling plants but from the side shoots that develop on a mother plant during the winter months. Unless artichokes find the climate to their liking, they may rarely produce side shoots and never produce harvestable heads. Artichokes do not like extreme hot or extreme cold; too much of either results in dormancy or death.

The true artichoke is finicky, but the Jerusalem artichoke is quite the opposite. It is a perennial sunflower that develops fat, edible roots. In the summer, the plants have no trouble reaching 15 feet in height, and the large, yellow, daisylike flowers are attractive in cut arrangements. In many areas, Jerusalem artichokes are so eager to grow that they can often be seen in ditches and waste areas. The roots are harvested in the winter after the plants die back and the soil has become chilled. To keep the plants from overtaking your garden, take care to pick up every last root. Those that are too small to peel and eat can be replanted immediately or anytime until mid-spring (they will keep just fine left buried in the ground). Alternatively, you can grow Jerusalem artichokes in some isolated spot, dig the roots as you want them in the winter, and let them come back on their own in the spring, like the true perennials they are.

ASPARAGUS

Varieties: No strains of asparagus are particularly talented at tolerating the stresses of hot weather, but all modern varieties resist rust and tolerate fusarium wilt, which may offer hope to lovers of these tender spears. The bad news about asparagus is that yields per square foot are quite modest, so you have to grow a lot of it if your appetite for asparagus is insatiable. Try 'Jersey Giant' or another updated strain to improve your chances of success.

Seasons: Asparagus is a perennial, planted from purchased roots in the dead of winter while they are dormant. Because a period of cold weather is required to lull the plants into dormancy, they do not do as well in Zones 9 and higher as they do in cooler areas. The edible parts are the young shoots that emerge in late winter and early spring.

Tips:

* Asparagus plants resemble huge ferns and are pretty enough to enhance the appearance of the landscape.

* In warm damp climates, excellent drainage is required, or the roots will rot.

* In Zones 7 and warmer, if the plants fail to produce well when harvested in spring, you can try turning their life cycle upside down by cutting the plants off at the ground in midsummer, mulching over them heavily, and keeping them rather dry until fall. Then, when the weather has cooled in late fall, water them heavily and harvest the spears as they pop through the mulch. If you handle them this way, don't harvest more spears in the spring; the plants will need those branches to recover their strength.

BEANS

Varieties: Virtually all beans are welcome additions to warm-climate gardens. Avoid old varieties unless you've already tasted them from someone else's garden. Modern varieties are much more productive and disease resistant, and the pods are larger and less stringy. Pole beans taste better than bush beans, but both types deserve planting. Among snap beans, state-of-the-art varieties include 'Derby' (bush snap), 'Slenderwax' (bush yellow snap), and 'Kentucky Blue' (pole snap). Where you desire good looks, try a variety that develops purple or streaked pods (the color fades to green when you cook them).

Lima beans love hot weather and often are more pest-resistant than snap beans. Both bush and pole varieties are available. For best flavor, harvest limas when the pods are well filled and have just begun to dry out. Shelling small limas is slow and time-consuming. Pole limas, especially varieties that bear very large beans, are the most productive.

Seasons: To ensure continuous production, arrange plantings like this:

> **Early spring:** Plant bush snap beans. If space permits, make two or three successive sowings two weeks apart.

Mid-spring: Plant pole snap beans or limas on a trellis and bush shell beans or bush limas in rows.

Late summer: Plant bush snap beans again.

Tips:

* For maximum water conservation, plant all beans in double rows, mulch heavily, and irrigate between the two rows.

* Very hot weather may ruin flowers and subsequent fruit set in bush snaps. When this happens, consider the beans a nitrogen-fixing cover crop and promptly turn them under.

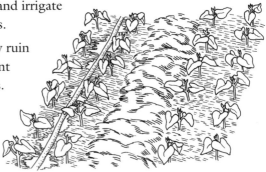

Soaker hose laid in the middle of a double row of beans and heavy mulch between rows

* In the Southeast, harvest shell beans when they are still green and freeze them. Insects usually infiltrate the pods by the time they are dry.

* In all areas, expect problems from Mexican bean beetles (see more about this pest on pages 177-178).

BEETS

Varieties: Beets are strictly a cool-weather crop, but they won't germinate in cold soil and can't take hard freezes. Choose a variety that matures quickly, such as 'Early Wonder' or 'Red Ace'. All varieties that bear edible roots also bear delicious, mild-flavored greens with a buttery texture. If the greens are your favorite way to eat beets, pluck them a leaf at a time while the plants are young. More tops will quickly appear.

Seasons: Fall and spring.

Tips:

* Make two small sowings two weeks apart to ensure a long harvest season.

* The best pickings come from plants that grow quickly and without stress.

* Cook beets unpeeled, and the skins will slip off easily.

* Accent chilled marinated beets with gingerroot for a fine culinary experience.

BRASSICAS

Types: Broccoli, cabbage, cauliflower, kohlrabi, collards, and kale are closely related. They share similar cultural requirements, with small differences in cold hardiness and pest resistance. Collards and kale are the most cold hardy and pest resistant of the group. Kohlrabi plants are the smallest and make the best use of limited space.

Varieties: Except with collards and kale, always choose very fast-maturing varieties such as 'Premium Crop' broccoli, 'Golden Acre' cabbage, 'Snow Crown' cauliflower, and 'Grand Duke' kohlrabi. All are heavy feeders that don't do well in extremely acidic soil. Enrich planting sites with compost or rotted manure, and water regularly. Always rotate brassicas with other crops to avoid problems with root maggots and soil-borne diseases.

Seasons: All brassicas are cool-weather crops grown only in early spring, fall, and winter.

For spring, start seeds indoors eight weeks before your last frost date. Set out the plants, under milk jug cloches, when they have six true leaves. (They will be five to six weeks old.) Kohlrabi and cauliflower grow quickly enough to be direct-seeded under hoop tunnels covered with clear plastic or fabric row cover. All brassicas should be in the ground, growing as stocky seedlings, by the time the last spring frost rolls around. Use a Bt insecticide to control cabbageworms and cabbage loopers from mid-spring on.

For fall, start cabbage, broccoli, cauliflower, and kohlrabi seeds indoors eight weeks before the first frost is expected. If you want to try brussels sprouts, this is the time to do it. With all these brassicas, you will be starting cool-natured plants while the weather remains decidedly summerlike. Keep the plants indoors under lights if you can, or fashion a row cover tent and move them into partial shade outdoors. If the plants are left unprotected, bugs will appear out of nowhere and eat them before their roots ever touch solid ground. Continue using row cover after the plants are set out, a couple of weeks before your first frost date. Collards and kale may be direct-seeded in early fall. Since they are quite winter hardy, a head start indoors is not necessary.

For winter crops in Zones 9 and 10, start seeds indoors in October and set out plants in late November.

Tips:

* Do try kohlrabi, which is very easy to grow.

* After the central head is harvested from broccoli, a number of edible side shoots will emerge from the main stem.

* In Zone 7, make heavy use of kale, the hardiest of all the brassicas.

* When overwintered, collards and kale develop flower buds in early spring. Harvest them before the flowers open, cook briefly, and enjoy.

CANTALOUPES

Varieties: Hybrids such as 'Luscious Plus' resist fusarium wilt and powdery and downy mildews, all of which can cause problems in warm climates. Older, open-pollinated strains such as 'Golden Gopher' and 'Edisto' also often are quite tough, and older varieties tend to have delicious aromas. Honeydew melons are cantaloupes with light green flesh and are trickier to grow than orange-fleshed cantaloupes. Other melons, including cushaws and casabas, are grown like slow-maturing cantaloupes.
Seasons: Spring and late summer. Traditionally, cantaloupes are direct-seeded in warm climates, but you can start them

> ### GIVE THEM ELBOW ROOM
> All vegetables should be spaced so that the leaves of neighboring plants barely touch one another. Although it feels mean at the time, thinning often is the kindest thing you can do for your vegetables. Thin early and often so that each plant gets adequate light and water and has room for expanding roots.

in peat pots and set them out when they are three weeks old if you're careful. Cantaloupes require warm weather. They taste best when they get plenty of water until the fruits are set and then little water thereafter.

Tips:

* To keep cucumber beetles, squash bugs, squash borers, and the little bugs that carry viruses at bay, keep melon plants covered with floating row cover until the first female blossoms appear (about thirty-five days).

* When fruits begin to swell, place folded newspaper beneath each one to keep soil-borne pests from boring into the fruits.

* Avoid mangling the vines when hand-weeding (see "Mulching Melons" on page 96).

* When each vine is holding a couple of melons, pinch back the ends of runners to encourage bushy growth, which will save space and shade ripening fruits.

* Harvest most varieties when the stem begins to "slip" from the melon when you give it a gentle tug. If the fruit remains attached when you pull, it probably isn't ripe. The color of the rind (beneath the netting) will often turn from green to yellow when the melons are ripe.

Protect maturing cantaloupe from pest damage by placing several thicknesses of newspaper under it.

CARROTS

Varieties: Choose a type that fits your soil: short, blunt ones in clay or longer ones in sandy loam. In the humid Southeast, where leaf spots threaten, choose a variety that resists alternaria, such as 'Seminole'. Variety and soil combine to give carrots their flavor. Experiment until you find a favorite.

Seasons: Direct-seed in early spring. Cover the seedbed with boards, thick folds of newspaper, or an old blanket for three days to keep it moist and to promote fast, uniform germination. A second planting can be made in early fall, but you will need to presprout the seeds between several thicknesses of wet paper towel, as they do not germinate well in hot soil.

Tips:

* Harvest all carrots in early summer and store them in the refrigerator, or soil-borne insects will move in.

* Where nematodes are not a problem, fall-sown carrots may be dug all winter.

* If rootknot nematodes are present, soil must be solarized before you can grow carrots. (For information on how to solarize see page 182.)

* Where the carrot rust fly is a common pest, grow carrots under floating row covers.

CHAYOTE

Varieties: Also called mirliton, chayote is a perennial cucurbit grown only in warm climates where the roots will not freeze in winter. Most gardeners get their start with fruits purchased at the supermarket. When kept in a warm place, the large, round end of the chayote fruit will produce a bud. Sprouted fruits are planted on their sides, with the sprouted end low and the pointed end barely covered with soil. The first year after planting, production of fruits is modest, but after that, fruit set becomes very heavy when days shorten in the fall, with some plants producing more than one hundred fruits. The vines are robust and decorative and are often grown on overhead trellises or fences.

Seasons: Plant sprouted fruits in mid-spring, when the soil is warm. For good pollination, plant at least two, spaced 6 to 12 feet apart.

Tips:

* Store chayote fruits in the refrigerator or another cool place to keep them from sprouting.

* The flesh is cooked and eaten like squash.

* In cold-winter areas, provide good insulation for the roots by mulching heavily after the vines die back in late fall.

CHINESE CABBAGE

Varieties: All types of Chinese cabbage, including the tall michihli types, the barrel-shaped wong boks, and the loose-headed bok choys are very easy to grow where days are short and cool. Where downy mildew and viruses threaten, choose resistant varieties such as 'Blues' and 'Springtime II'.

Seasons: Stick with the fall to winter season for this crop, for all Chinese cabbages bolt quickly when exposed to long days or prolonged warmth. If the soil is too warm to allow good germination, start seeds indoors and set plants out when the weather cools in mid-fall.

Tips:

* Harvest early and often to keep the young plants thinned so that the leaves of one plant don't touch the leaves of others.

* Plenty of water will help the heads grow quickly.

* When the heads reach full size, harvest and refrigerate them, as mature Chinese cabbage does not hold well in the garden.

* If aphids become a problem, spray the plants twice with insecticidal soap, then cover with floating row cover to keep the bugs from coming back.

CORN

Varieties: Most gardeners like to grow sweet corn. There are many different kinds, including hybrids, supersweets, and those with special genes that delay the transition of sugar to starch in the kernels. 'Silver Queen' is a popular favorite, but do try others, including bicolors. All varieties mature quickly when days are getting longer in spring and grow more slowly as days get shorter in late summer and fall. Varieties described as supersweet should be grown away from other varieties so they don't cross-pollinate. If they do, the flavor and texture of both plantings may be ruined.

Seasons: Plant every three weeks throughout the spring and early summer. A late crop may be planted in midsummer.

Tips:

* Plant in blocks rather than long rows so the wind can do a good job of spreading pollen from plant to plant. In small

plantings, you can help the pollination process further by sprinkling pollen from the tassels of one plant onto the silks of another.

* In windy areas, plant corn in furrows and pile up soil around the base of each plant before mulching.

Corn planted in furrows

* Mulching corn is laborious, but it keeps down weeds and saves time watering. In arid locations, a mulch can also raise the humidity level in the corn patch if you wet it down before dark. Increasing the humidity this way (in arid climates only) often helps promote good pollination.

Cucumbers

Varieties: In humid areas, look for excellent disease resistance in the varieties you choose. 'County Fair' and 'Marketmore' are among the most disease-resistant varieties. Others described as burpless and nonbitter taste great and

are of little interest to cucumber beetles. Heirloom cucumbers, including 'Armenians', perform very well in hot, arid climates. Expect all cucumbers to be rather short-lived, and plant them two or three times to ensure a steady supply. Compact bush-type cucumbers may be interplanted among tomatoes, okra, or sunflowers. When summer gets really hot, cucumbers like a little shade.
Seasons: Plant in the spring, just after the last frost, and again a few weeks later. For the last planting, sow seeds at least sixty days before the first fall frost is expected. In general, cucumbers are less tolerant of heat than their squash and cantaloupe cousins.

Tips:

* Use plenty of compost or rotted manure when planting cukes, and provide water regularly after blossoms appear.

* Drought stress can lead to insufficient pollination (fruits with shrunken blossom ends) and bitter flavor.

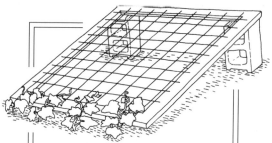

* Cucumbers tend to overproduce, so don't get carried away with the size of your plantings.

* Cukes have many insect enemies, but judicious use of floating row cover will outsmart them.

* Once cucumbers reach maturity and produce fruits for a few weeks, they die.

CUCURBITS ON FRAMES
Cucumbers and small-fruited melons produce better when they are trellised. If you don't have a chain-link fence or other ready structure, try growing them on frames. Build a wooden frame and attach a piece of 6-inch-mesh concrete-reinforcing wire to the frame. Prop one end of the frame on concrete blocks and plant cucumbers at the other end. As the vines grow, train them to sprawl over the frame. This is especially helpful with long-fruited varieties, which get kinky when grown on the ground. A tomato cage, opened into an arch and placed over young plants, also makes a good low trellis for cukes.

EGGPLANT
Varieties: The big bulbs found in most supermarkets grow well enough, but small-fruited varieties are easier to manage in the kitchen (you get more fruits of smaller size). Oriental varieties that produce long, cylindrical fruits are as easy to grow as other varieties.

CREATE A TOMATEGG

If you slice them right, you can graft an eggplant onto a tomato rootstock. If the tomato used is resistant to nematodes and verticillium wilt, the eggplant graft will be able to take advantage of that resistance.

Use healthy six-week-old seedlings (good bedding plants are fine). Use a razor blade or sharp knife to cut the top off the tomato just above the seedling leaves. Cut a -inch deep vertical slice through the center of the tomato stump, trim the bottom of the eggplant stem to a point, and fit the two together. Secure the graft with a strip of cloth tied tightly. Keep the patient in a protected place for two to three weeks, repotting it if necessary. Set it out when the graft union is quite solid.

Seasons: Early and late summer. Start the seeds indoors in early spring and set out the plants when they are six weeks old. Cover them with row cover for a couple of weeks to give them time to get established before flea beetles find them. Where frosts are rare, eggplant can be grown as a short-lived perennial with slight winter protection.

Tips:

*   If the combined stresses of verticillium wilt, nematodes, and flea beetles prove too much for your eggplant crop to handle, try growing plants in containers (in heat-sterilized soil) placed on a high bench or table where flea beetles won't find them.

FENNEL

Varieties: The vegetable known as fennel and the herb known as fennel are two different plants. The herb is grown exactly like dill. The vegetable, also known as Florence fennel or finocchio, includes the varieties 'Zefa Fino', 'Romy', and 'Herald'. When mature, it forms a bulb just above the ground.

Seasons: Plant Florence fennel in fall only. Sow seeds in flats in late summer, keep in partial shade, and set out after the soil has cooled.

Tips:

* Although Florence fennel loves cool weather, it is easily damaged by frost. Cover plants with an old blanket if a hard freeze is expected before you are ready to pull them.

* Fennel is often used to stuff fish.

GARLIC

Varieties: You can plant sprouted cloves from bulbs bought at the grocery store, often with good results. But if you truly love the bud, survey carefully selected strains offered by seed retailers and sample subtle variations in size, flavor, and aroma. Let your trial garlics grow for two years before choosing a favorite, as it may take more than a year for a strain to adjust to your garden. After you find a garlic you love, switch to biennial or perennial culture.

Seasons: Biennial. Plant cloves in the fall and harvest bulbs in early summer. The yield is generally highest when garlic is grown in rows that are replanted every fall, but garlic also can be managed as a self-perpetuating perennial clump. Dig off a different side of the clump each summer, leaving one-fourth of the bulbs undug.

Tips:

* When handled as a biennial, garlic can be easily rotated with bush beans.

* Garlic is very well adapted to warm climates because it is dormant during the hot summer months.

GINGER

Varieties: A tropical root crop, ginger is a wonderful plant to grow in containers placed in the shade. It requires a long season of warm, humid weather and is ideal for courtyards and patios. Ginger can also be grown in the ground, but it must have a rich, moist, well-drained, shady site.

Seasons: Start plants from sprouting root pieces found at the grocery store in late winter. Cut the roots into 1- to 2-inch pieces, allow the cut ends to dry, and plant them 1-inch deep.

Tips:

- ✳ Harvest roots from container-grown plants in the fall, or bring them indoors during the winter and harvest some roots when you repot the plant in the spring.

- ✳ Use fresh chopped or grated ginger in Oriental dishes or as a seasoning for beets and other root crops.

GOURDS

Types: Grown primarily for fun rather than food, most gourds fall into one of three botanical groups: *Cucurbita, Lagenaria, and Luffa.*

The small, brightly colored gourds classified as *Cucurbita pepo* are of the same species as summer squash and pumpkins. The fruits have tasteless interiors and boldly marked, often warted, hard rinds. Commonly sold as ornamental gourds, these are grown exactly like winter squash.

Hard-shelled gourds *(Lagenaria* species*)* include most of the brown, hollow gourds, in various shapes and sizes, used to make dippers, clubs, birdhouses, and endless craft items. One strain, the cucuzzi or Italian, is edible. My grandmother used to grow it every year in coastal Mississippi; she picked the young fruits and used them like zucchini. Scientists warn, however, against eating any old *Lagenaria* gourd, as some contain bitter compounds that can make you sick. If it tastes bitter, spit it out. Selected trustworthy cucuzzi seeds are available from some seed savers and members of the American Gourd Society (see addresses in chapter 8).

Luffas are known as dishcloth gourds, sponge gourds, or in some parts of the Southeast, vining okra. Okraesque selections usually have ridges, while others are rounder and smoother. Luffas may be eaten when very young and green but are usually left to ripen on the vine until dry. They are then soaked for a few hours, stripped of their skins, cleaned, and redried to be used as stiff sponges. I have seen Luffa vines used very effectively as a summer sunscreen for a greenhouse frame, which the owners covered with plastic in the winter. Luffas are very easy to grow in warm climates, and their culture is the same as *Lagenaria* gourds.

> **ADOPT A WILD GOURD**
> Several strains of gourds grow wild in Arkansas, Texas, and California. To identify which botanical group these wildings most closely resemble, look at the flowers. *Cucurbita* flowers are yellow and open in the daytime. *Lagenaria* flowers are white and open mostly at night.

Slices of *Luffa* or long, cylindrical *Lagenaria* gourds can be used like peat pots for starting seeds indoors. Cut them crosswise into 2-inch-thick slices, remove the seeds (and some of the inner membrane of *Luffas*), and place them cut side down in a shallow pan or tray. Fill the rounds with potting soil, dampen them thoroughly, and plant your seeds. When the seedlings are ready to transplant, set them in prepared holes with the gourd "pots" intact.

Culture: All *Lagenaria* gourds are grown the same way, and all have long, rampant vines. They can tolerate no frost and need a long, hot growing season. Plant them in the spring in a rich, well-drained spot. I start thinking about where to plant gourds in the fall and pile garden debris there, layered with a little soil and manure. In spring, I dump a handful of seeds into the pile of rotted stuff and then stand back. Once gourd vines get going, they can easily grow 6 inches a day, rapidly covering an old fence, slope, or anything in their path. For this reason, thin to only a few plants — three should be enough. As long as the vines are not too rank, you can allow them to wander beneath corn, okra, or caged tomatoes. *Lagenaria* gourds have very deep roots but do need supplemental watering during severe droughts. The white flowers open only at night.

Leave the gourds alone until summer ends and the vines die. Then, leaving a couple of inches of stem attached, cut the gourds from the vine, and let them air-dry in a barn or storage building. By spring they should be dry enough to cut, sand, paint, sculpt, or whatever, and the seeds inside will be nicely cured for replanting.

GREENS

Types: This generic category includes mustard, rape, mustard-spinach, bok choy, and other cooking greens. All are incredibly nutritious. For more greens, see separate entries in the sections on Chinese cabbage, spinach, and turnips.

Varieties: Anything goes, provided you stick with the fall growing season. Each green tastes a little different, and cool weather is needed to bring out the best flavor.

Seasons: Fall only. In late winter and spring, lengthening days cause most greens to bolt before they reach full size.

Tips:

* If aphids or cucumber beetles are problems, cover greens with floating row cover to keep them out.

* Wait until nights get cool to start picking your greens, and water them often to promote fast growth.

* Don't plant too many, unless you like to eat cooked greens every day.

* Virtually all greens can be stuffed, like cabbage leaves, after they have been submerged in boiling water for a few seconds to make them more pliable.

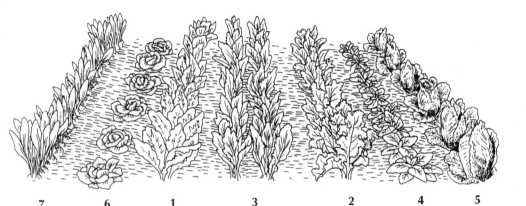

7   6   1   3   2   4   5

Planning a Greens Garden

In the fall, set aside a block of garden space for a greens garden. Assorted greens pack more nutrition per square foot than any other crops you can grow, and, with thoughtful planning, you can have a different green coming into its prime every week. Here's a way to grow seven types of greens in one block.

Prepare an 8-by-8-foot square, cultivate it well, and add a good helping of compost or manure. Begin planting by placing the slowest-growing, most cold-hardy greens — collards (1) and kale (2) — in parallel rows near the middle of the square. Leave enough space between them to plant a double row of turnips (3), which will be harvested by the time the collards and kale need the space.

On the outside of the kale, plant spinach (4) and Chinese cabbage (5). On the outside of the collards, plant lettuce (6) and beets (7). All these "outside" crops grow quickly and appreciate the shelter of their taller companions on cold nights. By the time winter sets in, you will have nothing left but greens that can take cold weather.

Try this level of greens diversity, and substitute greens you like for the ones I suggest, if our preferences differ. You will surely get more from seven types of greens than from a solid run of turnip or mustard.

Herbs

Every garden can host a special group of herbs that quickly become standard fare for the creative cook. Annual and biennial herbs fit nicely into beds and rows in the vegetable garden, but perennials need a place where they can grow for many years. The following herbs are very easy to grow in warm climates and are exceptionally useful in the kitchen. Master these, and then move on to more exotic selections if you have the time and space.

Annual Herbs

Basil is a warm-natured herb that matures very quickly, especially in spring and early summer when days are getting longer. For a continuous supply, start new plants three times — once in early spring, again in early summer, and a final sowing in early fall. Plant the seeds indoors and set plants outside when they have four leaves. Basil transplants very well and adapts to many types of soil. It needs at least half a day of sunshine. Large-leafed varieties are fine, but I like the delicate flavor of small-leafed basils such as 'Piccolo' and 'Greek Mini-Basil' best. Basil tastes best before it flowers.

Dill is very easy to grow from seeds sown directly in prepared soil. It needs plenty of sun and often requires thinning to keep the plants at least a foot apart. Dill matures quickly, so plan to make several sowings from spring until early fall. It can withstand light frosts but not hard freezes. If allowed to develop mature seeds, dill will naturalize with a little encouragement.

Savory develops into sparse little plants, but it's excellent for sowing among beans. The mild flavor is brought out by rich soil and regular watering. Plant it alongside spring and fall bush beans. Seeds can be started indoors, or you can direct-seed where you want the plants to grow.

Biennial Herbs

Chamomile has apple-scented blossoms that are welcome anywhere they pop up. A hardy annual, chamomile seeds do best when scattered atop prepared soil in fall and allowed to stand through the winter. In late spring, the blossoms may be dried for use in tea or allowed to self-sow.

Parsley has a reputation for slow germination, but you will always get a good stand by direct-seeding in the fall. Plants will bear slim pickings throughout the winter, and then explode with greenery in the spring. More plants may be started in the spring, although the best production comes from fall-seeded crops.

Sage is actually a perennial, but the best leaves (and flowers) come from plants grown as biennials. Start seeds in late summer and set them out in early fall. In subsequent years, propagate new plants by taking stem cuttings in late summer. These cuttings will quickly develop roots and grow into robust plants.

Perennial Herbs

Bay is winter hardy only in Zones 8 or warmer, but elsewhere it can be grown in large containers and brought indoors when hard freezes threaten. The small bush thrives outdoors in warmer areas and has few pest problems. Start with a purchased plant.

Chives are like tiny bunching onions. Seeds can be planted in the spring or fall, as the young plants like cool weather. The flowers are quite ornamental, making chives a good choice for container culture. Propagate in fall by pulling the clumps apart and replanting small clusters. Garlic chives form bulbous roots and beautiful white flowers in late summer. Dig and divide the bulbs in early fall.

Mint can be unruly and invasive, but jerking up excess mint is a joyous chore. Mintiness varies widely; stick with spearmint or peppermint for best results. Mint is very easy to start from seeds sown in early spring or from stem cuttings taken anytime. All mint types thrive in partial shade.

Oregano comes in many different strains, each with its own flavor and life cycle, but perennial Greek oregano is the most flavorful. This long-lived herb spreads close to the ground. It can be started from seeds, from runners that root in nearby soil, or from purchased plants. Plant it once, and you should have it forever.

Rosemary is winter hardy in most warm climates and can be grown as a clump or small hedge. Start with purchased plants (or a cutting from a friend). Cuttings root easily in a light potting medium, but seeds are slow to sprout and generally undependable. Full sun makes plants tight and bushy.

Tarragon is another herb that should be grown from cuttings rather than seeds. Procure plants in fall or late winter, as they grow best during cool weather and become semidormant in the heat of summer. Partial shade in midsummer also gives them welcome relief from heat stress.

Thyme comes in annual and perennial forms. The low, creeping perennials are useful landscape plants to grow between stepping-stones, and they taste great. Herb growers often offer beautiful variegated or golden-leafed strains. You can start seeds in late winter or fall, but to ensure good flavor, color, and form, it's best to start with purchased plants.

JICAMA

Types: A few species exist, but seeds for this root vegetable are sold simply as jicama. The plants are eerily similar to kudzu, with long, lush vines that run over anything in their path. The edible root forms late in the summer when days shorten and has the flavor and texture of a water chestnut.

Seasons: Sow seeds where you want the plants to grow after the last spring frost.

Tips:

* Best production of big roots results from more than six months of warm weather, regular watering, and pinching back of flower clusters when they appear in late summer. Dig the roots in early fall.

* The only way to fit jicama into a small yard is to train the vines over a fence, pergola, or overhead trellis, where they can provide fine summer shade.

LETTUCE

Types and varieties: Choose all varieties except pale icebergs, which are difficult to grow and low in nutrition. Leaf lettuces, such as 'Green Ice', are excellent, and Bibb types are easy and dependable. Soft-headed Bostons and frilly French lettuces are easily damaged by hail and heavy rain, so grow them mostly in the fall. Romaines mature somewhat slowly, so schedule them for fall, too. Some hardy varieties, such as 'Winter Density', remain in beautiful condition all winter when planted in mid-fall. If you can't decide what to plant, buy a mixture of seeds or make up your own blend of tempting varieties and sow them together in the same bed.

Seasons: Early spring, fall, and winter. Plant only a few square feet at a time, for a little lettuce goes a long way. Light is required for good germination, so pat the seeds into soft soil instead of burying them. For best germination, use fresh seeds.

Tips:

* As your lettuce grows, thin the plants often and eat the thinnings. When the leaves of one plant touch those of its neighbor, it's time to thin.

* Water the plants more as they grow larger. Lettuce has a high water content, and too little moisture can ruin its flavor.

* High temperatures can cause spring lettuce to turn bitter quickly, so check for flavor often and pull it up promptly.

OKRA

Varieties: Bushiness varies according to variety, as does the size and color of the pods. All varieties are very well adapted to warm climates, though none resist root-knot nematodes.

Seasons: Direct-seed in early summer and possibly again in midsummer for a robust fall crop. Seedlings are small and slow growing, but mature plants are extremely tough.

Tips:

* Plant okra next to sweet potatoes; the sweet potato vines will form a living mulch.

* Harvest okra pods daily, handle them gently to avoid bruising, and refrigerate them promptly. Cut the pods when they are less than 4 inches long.

* If the leaves make you itch, venture into the okra patch only when the leaves are dry and wear a long-sleeved shirt when cutting the pods.

* In late summer, top back (cut off the top third of) leggy plants to encourage the production of bearing side shoots.

* Okra makes a good hedge for low-growing crops that appreciate a bit of shade.

ONIONS

Types and varieties: Bulb onions are the most finicky members of this huge and eclectic group of wonderful plants. Big bulbs grow best when planted in fall for a spring harvest (roughly in Zone 8 south). Farther north, beware. Many onions are quite hardy, but when subjected to cold weather, they often decide to make seeds instead of bulbs. Irrigation is mandatory when growing bulb onions in dry areas, for drought stress makes them small and pungent rather than large and sweet. If you grow bulb onions, stick with short-day varieties.

Easy alternatives include leeks, scallions (green onions), multipliers, potato onions, and shallots. All are slow-growing cool-weather plants with very strong survival instincts.

Seasons:

Bulb onions. Plant purchased sets or plants in late winter for early summer harvest. In mild winter areas, they may be set out in late fall for spring harvest.

Leeks. Plant seeds in a flat in late summer and set out the plants in the fall when soil temperatures have cooled. Weed aggressively through the winter. In the spring, mulch heavily to encourage the development of long, white shanks.

Scallions. Sow fresh seeds in flats in late winter, early spring, and early fall for a continuous supply.

Shallots, multipliers, and potato onions. Plant bulblets or mother plants in fall and grow as biennials. Rotate the plot, replanting in a new place every fall to prevent the buildup of insects and diseases.

Tips:

* Save a corner of the salad patch for planting out purchased scallions rescued from rot in your refrigerator. Once situated in the soil, they will miraculously come back to life.

* Keep all onions well weeded.

PEANUTS

Varieties: Goobers can be a lot of fun to grow, especially for patient children. Dwarf or Spanish peanuts are easiest to fit into home gardens, but Virginia and jumbo types often show amazing vigor. The Virginia types are often regarded as the easiest ones to grow.

Seasons: Plant shelled, unhulled seeds in mid-spring after the soil has become warm. Plant them in wide, raised rows or in hills so that plants are at least 10 inches apart. Peanuts need frequent cultivation to control weeds and to keep the soil soft. Sandy soil enriched with organic matter is best. Maintain wide plant spacing to discourage foliar diseases.

Tips:

- After peanuts flower in midseason, pointed pegs curve down and plant themselves in the soil. These eventually become the peanuts. Wait to harvest them until the plants begin to fail in fall. Dig carefully, and allow the nuts to dry on the plants for two weeks.

- Set aside the small, immature nuts, wash them well, and boil them in salt water for a tasty snack.

Peas, Field

Types and varieties: These underappreciated legumes thrive in hot weather, when many other vegetables fail. They are strong nitrogen fixers and are therefore good to grow in poor soil. Small-seeded "lady" types have a wonderful buttery flavor, but by the time you shell them, the harvest may seem small. Large-seeded crowders, purple hulls, and black-eyes are more productive in terms of square-foot yields. Several new varieties developed by the USDA, including 'Bettergreen' and 'Bettergrow', are resistant to nematodes, cowpea cucurlios, and a leaf spot called cercospora.

Asparagus beans (also known as yard-long beans) are a long-vined, edible-podded field pea. They need high support, such as a 6-foot trellis or tepee, as the vines may reach 12 feet in length. Harvest asparagus beans when the pods are only a foot long for use as snap beans.

Seasons: Summer only. Make successive sowings from June through August. In the West, plant a large plot just before the summer monsoon season.

Tips:

- Use leftover seeds as a late summer cover crop.

- In the Southeast, where cowpea cucurlios are serious pests, harvest the peas when they are young and tender; freeze the excess.

Peas, Garden

Types and varieties: These are among the sweetest, most delectable morsels you can grow in your garden. They thrive in very cool weather, so opportunities to grow them well are severely limited in warm climates. Choose fast-maturing

varieties of the three common forms: shell peas, snow peas, and snap peas.
Seasons: Plant six weeks before the last spring frost or in midwinter where frosts are rare. Fall crops are iffy in Zone 7 but often do very well in Zones 8 and 9. Whether planting in the spring or fall, do not expect great germination unless the soil temperature is between 45° and 75°F. Soaking seeds overnight in water before planting often improves germination.

Trellis all peas.

Tips:

* Trellis all peas, regardless of what the seed packet says.

* When growing peas for the first time, inoculate the seeds with the appropriate nitrogen-fixing bacteria (order the bacteria with your seeds) to ensure fast, dependable growth.

* Peas do not like extremely acidic soil.

* Pick daily when the pods begin to swell, for pea quality deteriorates once peak conditions have been reached, especially in hot weather.

* In small gardens, dress up the outside of the row with leaf lettuce.

PEPPERS

Varieties: All varieties are nicely adapted to warm climates, so you can choose an assortment of shapes, colors, and flavors. Plant sweet peppers and hot peppers at opposite ends of the garden to limit cross-pollination. Large, thick-walled peppers may produce only a few fruits, while small, thin-walled ones will produce hundreds. Resistance to nematodes and a few other diseases is available. Some of the most dependable varieties include 'Sweet Banana', 'Anaheim', 'Gypsy', and 'Jupiter'. Among big bells, look for varieties such as 'Vidi' and 'Espana', that resist several viruses.
Seasons: Early and late summer. Large peppers often heat-check in midsummer, then resume heavy production in the fall.

Tips:

* Mulch heavily to conserve soil moisture, but keep the mulch pulled back 2 inches from the main stem.

* Stake most of your peppers to keep the fruits from touching the soil (an invitation to insects and disease).

* Choose a few plants to keep into early winter and leave those unstaked so they will be easy to cover with a blanket on frosty nights.

Stake peppers and mulch them well.

POTATOES

Types and varieties: Potatoes are another cool-weather crop to grow at least once a year, in spring, and possibly again in the fall. Choose fast-maturing varieties such as 'Pontiac' or another red-skinned variety that can be harvested small, as new potatoes. Fingerlings produce small but delicious yields. Big bakers are hard to grow in warm climates because they require an extended cool season.

Seasons: Plant cut-up seed potatoes in early spring, about two weeks before the last frost, and cover with 3 inches of soil and a mulch of straw or weathered leaves. Sprouted potatoes from the spring harvest may be planted in early fall for a small second crop.

Tips:

* If you allow seed potatoes to "green up" and develop fat sprouts before planting them, they will emerge much faster.

* Mulch potatoes very heavily to keep sunlight

HELPING PEPPERS GO PERENNIAL

Peppers are really perennial plants, and if you live where winters are mild, you can easily keep plants for two or even three years. In mid-fall, choose a few healthy plants, preferably varieties that produce small fruits. When most of the fruits have been harvested, prune back the tops by one-half, dig up the plants, and replant them in containers. Leave them sitting in the garden unless a hard freeze threatens. Bring them indoors if the weather becomes bitterly cold.

Begin feeding the peppers every two weeks with a weak liquid fertilizer in late winter, and then replant them in early spring. New growth should appear with the first hot days, and you'll be picking peppers from the overwintered plants when this year's seedlings are just setting fruits.

from reaching the potatoes (the tubers push upward as they grow).

* Do not eat potatoes that turn green after being exposed to sunlight.

* Expect to see Colorado potato beetles on spring plantings, and possibly blister beetles as well. (See pages 174-175 for controls.)

* Store potatoes indoors in a dark, cool, dry place.

PUMPKINS

Varieties: All pumpkins require quite a bit of space, and they are rampant ramblers. Small pie pumpkins are somewhat compact, though no really good pumpkins grow on a bush. Older open-pollinated field pumpkins are often very tolerant of disease and drought. Hybrids usually are faster to mature and more uniform in size and color. Miniature pumpkins, such as 'Jack Be Little', are prolific but not very tasty; use them like ornamental gourds.

Seasons: Pumpkins can be grown in spring (they will be ready to eat in midsummer), but they are normally grown for fall harvest, which means planting them in midsummer.

Tips:

* Pumpkin vines provide surprisingly good coverage for erodible slopes.

* Seeds often survive composting and become garden volunteers.

* The easiest way to grow pumpkins is to plant them in an abandoned compost heap and allow them to roam around the edge of the garden. Or, you can interplant them with corn or okra.

RADISHES

Varieties: Grow fast-maturing, little round salad radishes, such as 'Fuego', alongside lettuce in spring, then use them later as bug-deterrent row markers for summer squash. In fall, add daikons to your planting list if you like them. Beware: many daikons grow to several pounds.

Seasons: Early spring and fall for the best tasting ones. Radishes will grow in hot weather, but their flavor may be hot, and their texture woody.

Tips:

* Check radishes daily after a month and harvest as soon as they reach picking size.

* Dry weather followed by heavy rain can cause radishes to split.

* Radishes make great row markers for separating plantings of lettuce and other greens in the spring and fall.

* Kids love to harvest radishes, even if they don't like to eat them.

SALSIFY

Varieties: A relative of the dandelion, salsify develops a white carrotlike root that tastes a little like oysters when peeled and cooked. The only widely available variety is 'Sandwich Island Mammoth', rated at 120 days to maturity. When planted in early fall and harvested in spring, salsify may take as long as 150 days to develop fat roots.

Season: Biennial only. Direct-seed in late summer in Zone 7 or early fall farther south. Harvest in the spring before the tops elongate and form flower heads. The flowers are an attractive light purple color.

Tips:

* Plant salsify clusters rather than rows so you can dig the roots a clump at a time.

* Eat them steamed with butter, or mash the cooked roots and make them into mock oyster croquettes.

SPINACH

Types and varieties: Choose freely from varieties with smooth, semicrinkled or deeply crinkled leaves. Hybrids like 'Fallgreen' and 'Nordic' offer good disease resistance, which is especially important for fall crops. All spinach will grow nicely during the fall and winter in warm climates, provided the soil is well endowed with rotted manure.

The New Zealand and Malabar types are not spinaches at all, but they make a serviceable cooked spinach substitute in summer, when crisp-leaved spinach will not grow. New Zealand strains have the mildest flavor, but Malabars are more ornamental, some with distinctive red stems and leaf veins. Either type may be grown in large containers and allowed to sprawl over the edges.

Seasons: Fall is the preferred season for planting true spinach, which tastes best when sweetened by light frost. In many areas it can be picked all winter. Spring crops often do well where nights remain cool, but they will bolt quickly after a few warm days. The New Zealand and Malabar types are warm-season crops, planted in the spring and harvested during the summer.

Tips:

* Grow only in very fertile soil that has recently been manured or enriched with compost. If your spinach is spindly and yellow, improve the soil before you try to grow it again.

* Water often while the plants are young.

SQUASH, SUMMER

Varieties: All squash produce extremely well, and part of the fun of growing squash is trying different varieties. I grow only two plants of any variety at a time, but I usually grow at least three varieties in a small plot. If you don't save the seeds, you can even mix varieties in the same hill. Try unusual forms not normally seen in markets: round zucchini such as 'Gourmet Globe'; long, light green cocozelles; little multicolored scalloped squash like 'Sunburst'; and light green Lebanese strains.

Seasons: Plant in spring, just after the last spring frost, and again three weeks later. Sow a fall planting in late summer at least sixty days before the first fall frost.

Tips:

* Place a shovelful of compost below each hill.

* Pick ripe fruits early and often to help the plants produce more (and more and more).

* If the rind is hard and the seeds are as stiff as cardboard, the fruit is overripe. Compost it.

* Where virus and insect pressure is severe, grow summer squash under floating row cover until the first female flowers appear.

WINTER SQUASH

Varieties: Acorn squash, spaghetti squash, and delicata (sweet potato) squash are the same species as summer squash, *Cucurbita pepo*, but other winter squash are of several different species. These include buttercups *(C. maxima)*, which are huge plants with long vines and often regarded as having the best flavor and texture of all winter squash. Butternuts are *C. moschata*, and they seem to have fewer problems with many cucurbit pests. Within each group, stellar varieties include 'Jersey Golden Acorn', 'Orangetti' spaghetti squash, 'Delicata' sweet potato squash, 'Buttercup-Burgess' buttercup, and 'Ponca' or 'Zenith' butternut. Hubbard types hardly compare to these in terms of flavor. Regardless of species or variety, all winter squash require about three months to reach maturity. Acorn squash can be harvested early, before they are fully ripe.

Seasons: Plant in the spring for summer harvest or in late summer so they will mature before the first hard freeze. For the second crop, seeds may be started indoors and the plants set out when they are three weeks old. Keep plantings small, as winter squash are very productive.

Tips:

* Plant in an old compost heap, at the garden's edge, so the long vines can ramble down the edge of the garden.

* Delicatas have lovely stripes and variegations; they are ornamental, and the fruits are small enough to make it possible for them to hang on to a chain-link fence.

* When the rinds are hard and the vines are on the brink of death, cut the fruits with a bit of stem attached and store them indoors in a dry place.

* Storage time varies from two months for acorns to much longer for buttercups. I have had spaghetti squash that remained sound for a full year.

SWEET POTATOES

Varieties: 'Jewell' is widely available and easily grown, but many other varieties are worth searching for by following up classified ads in gardening magazines. The most updated varieties, including 'Excel' and 'Beauregard', taste great and resist several common insects and diseases.

Seasons: Plant slips — rooted stems that grow out of the ends of the potatoes — in late spring after the soil is warm. Start digging when the roots are the size you want, usually in early fall.

Tips:

> ✳ Allow sweet potatoes to cure in a warm, dry place for two weeks before storing them. This helps skin wounds to heal and seals them up nicely for long-term storage.

> ✳ Never refrigerate sweet potatoes; it causes them to rot.

Swiss Chard

Varieties: These decorator greens are available with snow-white ribs or ruby-red ones, and several seed suppliers offer mixtures of both types. Dwarf forms are now becoming available, too.

Seasons: Spring and fall. Chard is the best green to grow during the in-between times when cool-natured greens either bolt or taste bad due to warm temperatures or long days. Four or five chard plants will provide plenty of pretty greens when harvested a leaf at a time.

Tips:

> ✳ Provide plenty of water while the plants are young and grow them in rich, well-drained soil in full sun. Gradually thin the plants to 8 inches apart and eat the thinnings.

> ✳ Because chard plants are so attractive, grow them along your garden's most visible edge.

Tomatillos

Varieties: The tart husked tomatoes known as tomatillos may be tall bushes or low, sprawling vines. The upright form, *Physalis ixocarpa*, has larger fruits than the "ground cherry," which is classified as *P. peruviana*. Either or both grow well in warm climates, as they require a long warm growing season to produce well. The biggest harvest comes in late summer and fall.

Seasons: Plant seeds in the spring and set out plants after the soil is warm. After your first year growing tomatillos, look for volunteers and transplant them to where you want them to grow.

Tips:

* Like their close cousins tomatoes, tomatillos need a trellis or cage to keep them off the ground.

* Culture is the same as for tomatoes, but tomatillos require less water.

* Harvest the fruits when they are mature but green. Chop and freeze them for salsa.

TOMATOES

Varieties: Look for a high level of disease resistance, as tomatoes are at high risk for many diseases when grown in warm climates. The most pressing ones are verticillium wilt (V), fusarium wilt (F), root-knot nematodes (N), and tobacco mosaic virus (T). More than one *F* after a variety name means it resists two races of fusarium. An *A* indicates resistance to alternaria stem canker, a minor disease that is different from the alternaria commonly known as blight.

Besides disease resistance, consider whether varieties are determinate or indeterminate. Determinate varieties have a bushy habit and load up with fruits all at once. After the fruits ripen, the plants usually decline, but may make a modest comeback. Determinate varieties need no pruning and are great for canning, freezing, or selling. Also, a robust determinate tomato covered with ripening fruits is a beautiful sight to see. The only trick to growing determinate varieties in a warm climate is to plant them early so the flowers will set fruits before the weather becomes extremely hot.

Indeterminate tomatoes develop longer vines and numerous suckers, or side shoots, which develop into bearing branches. Most gardeners prune off some of these suckers to keep the plants shapely, but you don't have to. In warm climates, never prune an indeterminate plant to a single stem as gardeners do up north. The fruits will burn in the sun and ripen unevenly.

Many gardeners think that indeterminate tomatoes taste better than determinate ones, but that's a subject to take up with your neighbors over the backyard fence. Tomato flavor results from an interaction of soil, variety, and growing conditions. In taste tests, people traditionally give the highest ratings to varieties with a high sugar content.

In case all this is too confusing, here are some top varieties that seem to grow well wherever they are planted. 'Celebrity' (VFFNTA, determinate) has top disease resistance and excellent flavor. Other popular varieties include

'Better Boy' (VFN, indeterminate), 'Bigset' (VFN, determinate), 'Mountain Delight' (VFFA, determinate), and 'Lemon Boy' (VFN, indeterminate), which bears yellow fruits. 'Early Cascade' (VF, indeterminate) and 'Red Cherry' (not rated for resistance, indeterminate) often continue to set fruits in hot weather when other tomatoes heat-check. In arid locations, 'Pearson' (not rated for resistance, indeterminant) remains a favorite.

To keep things interesting, grow two plants of each of several different varieties and colors. Six healthy plants will bear a lot of tomatoes (more than enough for two people to eat and give away). Also, it's worth noting that some old varieties that are not rated for resistance really are resistant to a number of diseases and disorders. Among heirlooms, small-fruited varieties are often the safest bets.

Seasons: Spring to fall. For continuous production, plan to set out tomatoes three times: mid-spring, early summer, and late summer. Tomatoes set out after the weather turns warm seem to have fewer problems with early blight — another good reason to stagger your planting dates. You can root cuttings off the first planting and keep them in containers in partial shade, then set them out in late summer for fall production.

Tips:

* Dawn-to-dusk sun is often too much for tomatoes in warm climates. Full morning sun is mandatory (to prevent foliar disease), but only a few hours of midday or afternoon sun give plants a welcome break.

* Use your best compost when planting tomatoes. Work two heaping shovelfuls into the soil beneath each plant, and then set the plants deeply, so that only a few leaves are sticking out above the soil.

* Use cutworm collars (see page 176) around precious seedlings you have raised from seeds.

* Milk jug cloches (see page 38), kept over the plants for a week or two in spring, help transplants adjust quickly.

* Mulch all tomatoes heavily with straw, grass clippings, or another organic mulch. Water copiously early in the season, then slack off when fruit production declines. If tomatoes become very dry, raise the moisture level of the soil gradually,

TOMATO CAGE TECHNIQUE

Tomatoes must be staked, trellised, or caged to keep them off the ground. When allowed to sprawl on the ground, they are subject to a number of diseases that don't bother them when they are held aloft.

Each method has its place. Thrifty little patio tomatoes often can be tied to a single stake, or you can use double stakes and keep a larger plant pruned to a columnar shape. This won't improve the crop, but it may make it possible to fit a few plants into a small space.

If a chain-link or chicken-wire fence is available, tomatoes can be tied to it with strips of cotton cloth or old hosiery. This works great with indeterminate tomatoes that you intend to keep all season, but it ties up your fence so you can't use it for other vining crops.

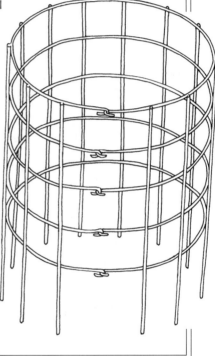

I keep a few tomato cages of varying sizes and would have much difficulty gardening without them. Besides using them to grow tomatoes, I use them in the winter as bins for collected mulch material and open out some to use as arching frames over beds that require coverage with blankets or plastic. Uncovered, the arches help keep dogs and kids from playing among new seedlings. My tomato cages are never unemployed. They are made of 6-inch mesh concrete-reinforcing wire cut into lengths varying from 4 to 7 feet. With heavy-duty wire snips, I trim off the crosswise pieces of wire on the bottom so that the verticals become "spokes," which I can push into the soil. I bend the horizontal tines on the sides and hook them around the wire on the opposite edge.

Tomato cages may topple over in late summer when they become topheavy with fruit. Although this does not kill the plants, it can be prevented by staking the bottoms of the cages with metal or wood stakes, driven into the ground at an angle. Or, install posts between cages and secure the tops of the cages to the posts with wire.

over a period of several days, to prevent fruit cracking (see page 42).

❋ In fall, cover plants with an old blanket if a frost or light freeze is predicted. When a hard freeze comes along, pick all the green fruits that seem to be almost ripe, bring them indoors, and set them in a warm place to ripen.

Turnips

Varieties: 'Tokyo Cross', 'White Lady', and 'Just Right' produce tasty greens and firm, white roots quickly and dependably. Many other varieties that bear red, purple, or yellow roots are available.

Season: Fall only. Sow directly in prepared soil in early to late fall, roughly forty-five days before the first frost is expected. In frost-free areas, plant in November so the plants can enjoy shortening, rather than lengthening, days. Turnips tolerate light frosts and will bear for a long time if you regularly harvest the oldest leaves from each plant. Both tops and roots are often ruined by hard freezes. If you want lots of turnip roots, make successive sowings in the fall two weeks apart.

Tips:

* Besides eating them smothered with hot sauce, with corn bread on the side, use young turnip greens as a spinach substitute in Italian recipes. Pasta stuffed with turnip greens and ricotta cheese is delicious!

* When the roots are ready, pull them, trim off the tops, and wash them before storing them in the refrigerator.

MULCHING MELONS

All melons tend to ripen unevenly when you accidentally mangle their vines. One side of a sabotaged melon may be overripe, while the other side will lack color and flavor. If the vines are likely to be twisted during hand-weeding, it may be better to leave the weeds alone.

The best strategy is to prevent weed problems by double-mulching melons just before they begin to run, using folded newspaper or sheet plastic on top of the soil, which is then covered with straw, leaves, or some other organic matter. Cultivate out all the weeds before laying down the mulch, then stay out of the melon patch until the fruits are ripe.

Watermelons

Varieties: If you have a large space and deep, loamy soil, you can grow good watermelons. Small-fruited icebox types like 'Sugar Baby' and 'Minilee' take up a little less space, but all watermelons are rampant runners. Seedless watermelons must be started indoors, as they seldom germinate well when direct-seeded. Once they are off and growing, however, seedless watermelons are as easy to grow as seeded ones, and much more precious. 'Jack of Hearts' is a dependable, medium-size seedless variety. Plant it with 'Crimson Sweet' or another vigorous hybrid to ensure good pollination. Yellow-fleshed melons are grown just like those with red flesh, but they are seldom seen in stores because they do not ship well.

Season: Spring only. Watermelons need three months of warm weather to mature, and they must grow quickly and vigorously to escape problems with insects and diseases.

Tips:

* ✳ Figuring out when a watermelon is ripe can be quite a challenge. Frequently, birds are better thumpers than people. They will peck a few times at underripe melons and dig little holes in the rind when the melons approach full ripeness. The pale spot on the bottom of the melon will often turn yellow as ripeness draws near, and the rind will lose some of its glossiness. Err on the side of caution and wait a few days if you have doubts about a melon's ripeness.

ENJOYING THE HARVEST

One July a few years ago, a friend told me of a fantasy she had. She had been picking sweet corn to freeze (a project that had been going on for days) and wondered what would happen if she just lay down between the rows and went to sleep. Would anybody find her, or would she just die there? If you've ever been in that situation — when it's 95°F, the corn is ready and it won't hold, and you're the only Little Red Hen that can bring in the crop — you can understand this woman's unpleasant daydream. There are ways to avoid this nasty experience.

First, grow only what you really intend to eat, especially if you are gardening alone. Picking, cleaning, bagging, and giving away produce is extremely time-consuming, and it doesn't make much sense. When you keep plantings small and have something coming in and something going out at all times, you will have only a little to give away, which will make your gifts all the more precious to your friends and family.

Of course, there are exceptions. One man I know, who's in his eighties and has gardened all his life, still plants a huge garden, but members of his church come to help with the weeding and harvesting; he picks only what he wants to eat. Another friend always plants a little extra of easy crops, like squash, and trades the excess at a produce stand, taking home things like peaches and apples that he does not have growing in his own yard.

Still, I think you will enjoy your garden more if you grow only a little of the things you like best and adjust your palate so that you eat whatever is fresh at any given time. This can be a challenge, and it takes ongoing effort to learn interesting ways to prepare your garden's bounty. I recommend getting to know the cookbook section of your local library and making a habit of trying new dishes. I read cookbooks all the time and have run across some pretty strange stuff, like green tomato cookies, which I will never try. At the same time, it's through reading cookbooks that I learned that a lot of garlic is generally required in the best eggplant dishes and that many Italian, Greek, and Chinese chefs will gladly swap spinach for fresh young turnip greens.

Finally, be ruthless with any plant that doesn't please you, either because it gets sick, bugs love it more than you do, or it's old and deserving of a dignified death. When something fails, take it out. Then, turn that failure into opportunity by undertaking some quick soil-improvement maneuvers or filling the space with healthy young plants.

Chapter Four

SUN-PROOF FRUITS

MANY PEOPLE'S MENTAL PICTURES OF PARADISE include bushes and trees dripping with ripe, luscious fruits. Most of us would like our yards to be this way (I know I would), but just how close can you come to turning this dream into reality?

Depending on where you live, you may be surprised at how many fruits you can grow if you open your mind to unusual types that you've rarely seen, much less tasted. Oriental persimmons, figs, golden currants, autumn olives, guavas, and pomegranates are just a few of the strange fruits that grow well in warm-climate gardens. In addition, much-improved varieties of blackberries, strawberries, and grapes can bring such varied flavors to the home garden that you'll hardly miss high-maintenance apples or peaches that bear only once every three or four years.

But let me stop myself before I say "You can't" to any dream you have of growing a certain fruit. Maybe you can grow pie cherries, apricots, or some other fruit rarely recommended by Extension Service agents in warm climates. Maybe you can grow your dream — if you have the perfect site.

All fruits are site specific. That is, they have definite requirements for the right combination of exposure, winter chilling, soil moisture, and fertility, as well as often limited abilities to defend themselves against pests and diseases.

In warm climates, the lack of a long cold winter is one of the major limiting factors in the selection of growable fruits. Fruit specialists use the phrase *chill hours* when estimating how much cold a plant needs to ensure that it goes dormant, blooms, and sets fruits at the appropriate times. Loosely defined as the number of hours that wood temperature is below 45°F, chill hours vary tremendously with cultivars. Before you invest in an expensive fruit tree, make sure your location comes close to matching its chill requirement. In catalogs, varieties promoted as "low chill" generally are appropriate for mild winter areas.

The best way to begin selecting fruits for your yard is to check with your local Extension Service and find out which fruits are known to grow successfully in your area. Ask about both tree fruits (apples, plums, peaches, pears, and so on) and small fruits (mostly berries). When you talk with the agent or Master Gardener, be sure to ask about unusual fruits they have heard of being grown by other gardeners. If your neighbor can grow a certain fruit, so can you.

In the following pages, I discuss a dozen or so fruits that grow well in most warm climates and are ornamental enough to add to the visual beauty of your yard. Many other fruits may fit into special niches on your property. Still, it's best to start small and gradually add more fruits to your collection. Unless you have a large amount of space for an orchard or arboretum, choose two or three fruits that you want very badly and try to be content with those, at least for a while.

But first, let's consider the basics of fruit culture. Bear in mind that most fruits are long-lived, but they don't live forever. In warm climates especially, many fruits decline in vigor after a few years and need to be replaced. While there are exceptions, estimate the bearing life of small fruits at less than ten years. Longevity varies among tree fruits, from less than twenty years for plums and peaches to thirty years or more for Asian pears.

HOMEGROWN FRUITS

You can never just plant a fruit and then forget about it. They don't grow that way. Fruits need your help and guidance; without it, they will never be happy. In return, they can make you very happy indeed. Here are five basic steps to growing fruits successfully.

STEP 1: SELECT THE BEST SITES

Before you set your heart on any fruit, take a realistic look at what your yard has to offer. Start with the soil. Do you have nematodes? Acidic or alkaline conditions? Compacted subsoil or caliche? A little or a lot of shade? If any extreme situations exist, limit the fruits you intend to grow to species that can adapt to those extremes. Blueberries like boggy, acidic sites, while buffalo currants thrive on dry, windswept slopes. Where spring frosts linger a little too long, apricots will almost always lose their blooms, but late-blooming apples won't. Look for special niches suitable for small fruits — a warm, sheltered corner for figs or a comfortably sunny retaining wall for grapes or kiwis.

STEP 2: PREPARE PLANTING HOLES IN ADVANCE

It can be very upsetting to encounter a boulder or caliche deposit in the place you've picked for an expensive pair of trees that have already arrived and are past due for planting. Digging in advance spares you this nightmare and gives you a chance to recondition soil that's been covered with grass and is rich in grubs. If you are digging in fall for spring planting, it's okay to put a little manure or compost in the bottom of the hole and only partially refill it. At other times, limit soil conditioners to peat moss, well-seasoned compost, leaf mold, and other texturizers. Forget about fertilizers until the plants have developed sufficient roots to use them. The exception is extremely alkaline soil, which can be treated with modest amounts of soil sulfur or ammonium sulfate prior to planting young fruits. You may scatter lime into acidic soil as you excavate and refill planting holes.

STEP 3: MULCH AND REMULCH

Use mulch liberally to suppress weeds and keep moisture in the soil, but collect and replace organic mulches at least once a year to interrupt the life cycles of pests. The best time is in early winter, after the leaves have fallen from the plants. Clean up the space under fruit plants using a stiff rake, and then compost all the leaves, fallen fruits, and weed skeletons you collect. After leaving the area open for a few weeks to allow birds and other predators to work the site, start mulching anew with fresh materials such as straw, grass clippings, or shredded hardwood leaves.

When fruit-bearing bushes or trees reach their mature size, you can switch

A Primer on Planting

Planting trees and bushes in warm climates is similar to planting them in other places, with a few small differences. Those differences relate to the leaf-to-root ratio of the young plant. In warm climates, you must make sure that a young tree or bush starts its new life with a modest amount of top growth. This means starting with young plants and pruning them back severely when they are planted. During the first year, the plant's energy should be directed toward the development of extensive roots rather than a lot of leaves. After all, roots gather and hold moisture during hot, dry weather, while leaves are the main avenue through which that precious moisture is lost. Prune plants before you plant them so you won't have to stand on (and compact) the soil that surrounds fragile, freshly planted roots.

(A)

You may plant trees in fall (if you can find them). When you can get plants that are just going dormant, they can take advantage of winter rains when planted in fall. However, most nurseries dig and ship their plants in late winter. Always plant before the buds break and the first leaves appear. That way, roots can get situated before they must carry on the serious business of keeping leaves well provided with moisture and nutrients.

Instead of digging a deep, round hole that matches the size of the root ball, dig a wide, bowl-shaped hole, so that you can spread every root out as far as it will go. In areas where the soil will need to be substantially improved, you may need to dig a huge hole, nearly as big as the anticipated root zone of the mature plant. But unless you live where the soil is alkaline and very low in organic matter, a hole roughly twice the size of the root ball will do.

(B)

When you're through digging and have partially refilled the hole with soil mixed with compost and peat moss, check the depth to make sure it is right. Plant trees and bushes at the same depth they grew at the nursery (A). If you plant them too deep, you may sabotage a graft. Planting them too shallow exposes tender roots to hostile elements. When planting in an oversize hole, set the plant just a little high, as it will settle as the excavated soil compacts.

When you set the plant in the hole, spread the roots and refill the hole with a few inches of soil, or just enough to hold it in place. Flood the hole with water (B). Rearrange the roots, add a little more soil, and flood again. Continue this process until the hole is filled. The layering of soil and water helps guard against the possibility of air pockets around the roots and ensures that every bit of soil that touches the roots will be evenly moist. Stake the tree (C).

(C)

to a living mulch of clover or fescue, kept closely mowed. Don't try to remove every weed that clusters around the trunk or plant base, as you'll probably end up hurting the plant much more than a little weed possibly could. Fight hard to keep Bermuda grass from growing beneath all fruits, however, as it exudes chemicals that inhibit the growth of other plants.

Mulching is not recommended in some situations, such as when insects, mice, or other pests are encouraged by the presence of a mulch. If you opt to go mulchless, make an alternative plan for the orchard floor that will be of some benefit to the plants, such as planting it in nitrogen-fixing biennial yellow clover. The clover will die out in the summer, but with a little help, it will reseed itself in time for fall germination.

STEP 4: PRUNE THOUGHTFULLY

Trees must be trained into a strong sculpture, and many small fruits must have their old parts lopped off to prevent pests and diseases from taking hold. Pruning is the single most important thing you can do to give a fruit tree a fair chance. Prune annually, and never allow unbalanced limbs to grow out of control. Prune small fruits to allow excellent exposure to sunshine and fresh air.

Because winters in warm climates often are punctuated by spells of weather that feel like spring, it's usually best to do your pruning twice during the winter. The first pruning, in early winter, is to remove dead or diseased plant parts. Toward the end of winter, when new buds are beginning to bulge, do the major pruning to shape and reduce the plants' anatomy. If you do a lot of pruning early in the winter, a fake spring spell may coax the plants into blossoming too early. On the other hand, if you wait until spring has sprung, disease organisms will have an easier time entering juicy open wounds.

THE WELL-SHAPED TREE

Fruit trees are usually pruned to one of two shapes — a vase or a central leader.

The vase shape (A) is used for peaches, apricots, and plums, which need excellent penetration of fresh air and sunshine. See how the vase shape creates a weak point in the crotch of the tree? For this reason, vase-shaped trees must be thinned thoughtfully, or the weight of too many fruits will literally tear the tree apart.

The central leader shape (B) follows the natural tendencies of slow-growing apples, persimmons, and pears. With apples, branch spreaders are sometimes used to keep the limbs from crowding one another. When limbs are trained to angle outward rather than upward, they can handle more weight when loaded with fruits.

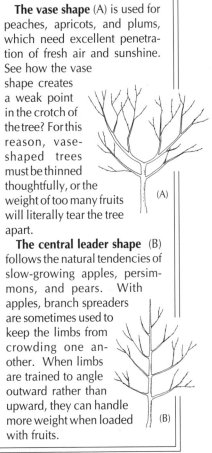

When pruning trees, always leave a little stub of each limb intact. The magic place to cut is about ¼ inch above the raised ring of bark that seems to wrinkle around the point where the limb joins the branch. This ring is called the collar, and it contains high concentrations of chemicals that mobilize themselves when the pruning cut is made. These chemicals form a restrictive interior wall that keeps out various invaders that try to enter through the cut. As long as the collar is left intact, there is no need for pruning paints or other wound dressings.

STEP 5: FERTILIZE AT THE RIGHT TIME

The flavor and nutrition content of fruits are radically affected by the vigor of the plants that produce them. Ideally, the area over any fruit plant's roots should be the site of continuous nutrient cycling, where manures and mulches are constantly decomposing, slowly enriching the soil that lies beneath. Some fruits, like figs, rarely need extra fertilizer, while others must have a boost now and then if they are to produce well, resist pests, and taste as fine as their genes allow.

In general, when fruit plants are old enough to bear, they are old enough to fertilize. In late winter, when the pruning has been done, fertilize berries, brambles, and trees with a 1-inch layer of composted manure and a dusting of cottonseed meal or some other slow-release organic fertilizer tucked under the mulch. Do it again when the fruits are half ripe. Never fertilize a plant that's on the verge of going dormant, or you'll risk stimulating tender green growth that will be killed by a minor hard freeze.

Many fruits can absorb some nutrients through their leaves, and it's cheap and easy to drench them with a liquid foliar fertilizer made from fish and kelp in mid-spring, when they are most likely to appreciate the nutrient banquet such products provide. But remember to do it on a cloudy day when the moisture from the spray will remain cool until it dries.

GETTING TO KNOW FRUITS

If you get passionately involved with any fruit, look to comprehensive reference books on fruit culture or special Extension Service bulletins for the fine points of selection, siting, pruning, and fertilizing. Local fruit aficionados are rich sources of information, but be forewarned: Each fruit has its own lingo, and you'll have to learn it before you can understand advice given by local experts. Where grapes or apples grow well, expect to hear many discordant opinions on how to grow them. Also remember that the methods that work best for commercial growers may not apply in your backyard. For example, you don't need working space for heavy spraying equipment, and a commercial grower would certainly scratch his or her head over an espaliered fig.

To whet your appetite for homegrown fruits, following is an introduction to the fruits most often recommended to gardeners in warm climates. I have divided them into small fruits and tree fruits. Fruits within these two groups have much in common in terms of space requirements, maintenance, and ease of culture.

SMALL FRUITS

Small fruits don't grow on trees; they grow on small plants, bushes, or vines. Small fruits and berries fit easily into small yards, and you can get much more variety out of limited space with these fruits than with those that grow on trees. Most small fruits are easy to grow and can be moved without too much trouble if the initial site proves unsuitable.

Don't get the impression that you are settling for less by growing small fruits rather than tree fruits, for the opposite is true. With few exceptions, the best small fruits are too delicate to ship and quite laborious to pick, so farmers seldom grow them on a commercial scale. Fresh figs are rarely seen in supermarkets, and the same goes for fully ripened strawberries or blackberries. Growing them yourself may be the only way to sample some small fruits, short of finding a local fruit hobbyist who has a generous nature.

The following small fruits adapt to a wide range of soils and microclimates. After we look at these main selections, I'll review some lesser-known small fruits that you may want to try in your garden.

BLACKBERRIES

Blackberries are very well adapted to most warm climates. Most prefer slightly acidic soils. In the East, improved varieties from Texas and Arkansas bear juicy berries much larger than wild strains and have a bushy, upright growth habit. The flavor is usually best in cultivars that have thorns. In the West, many of the best varieties are somewhat trailing, being improved descendants of tasty wild strains from the Northwest. When choosing varieties, consult your local Extension Service for recommendations. 'Shawnee' is a regional favorite in the Southeast, Texans love their 'Rosboroughs', and 'Cascade' and 'Olallie' are popular in the West.

All blackberries are easier to manage when restrained by a trellis or low fence. If none is available, it's easy to erect a T trellis, which also works well for red or gold raspberries.

All blackberries (and most other brambles) bear on one-year-old canes. In other words, those that come up green and lush one year will set fruits the following year. After the last berries have been picked, cut out old canes at ground level to short-circuit pests and keep the plants vigorous.

T-trellised blackberries

Various blackberry relatives are worth trying in Zones 7 and 8, including loganberries (big, sprawling bushes that bear tart fruits gradually over a period of weeks); boysenberries (sweet, aromatic fruits that are reddish like raspberries); and tayberries (a pure blackberry-raspberry cross that bears very early).

BLUEBERRIES AND HUCKLEBERRIES

Blueberries and wild huckleberries also like acidic soil that remains moist most of the year. They are native to lowlands and stream banks in the eastern United States but can be grown in the West, provided alkaline soil is reconditioned to make it more acidic. Add liberal amounts of ground bark, rotted leaves, or peat moss to the hole when planting blueberries where the soil is not naturally acidic. Or, grow a pair of blueberry bushes in a large half-barrel filled with an acidic potting mix. Train them into lovely arches that bear fruits in the summer and glow red in the fall.

Highbush blueberries, such as those grown in the Northeast and Northwest, have high water requirements and resent hot weather, but the rabbiteye types (developed mostly in Tifton, Georgia) can take summer heat and drought. Still, they require irrigation or regular watering through the first half of the summer while they are holding fruits. Improved rabbiteye cultivars are seldom bothered by pests and diseases.

More than one variety (of either type) is required for good pollination. By the time blueberries are five years old, three rabbiteye bushes should bear 5 gallons of fruits over a period of several weeks. If you are also growing blackberries, choose late-maturing blueberries so that the harvest periods will barely overlap.

Blueberries make an attractive hedge when planted in a short line, or you can grow them in a mound that can be covered with bird netting when the berries are almost ripe. Late-afternoon shade is often beneficial, so don't worry if the best place you can find is bordered by trees.

If you have wild huckleberries on your property, remove overhanging tree limbs to give them more light and clean out weeds and wild vines to reduce underground competition for nutrients and water. Huckleberries always set fruits, regardless of the weather, and are among the most trouble-free fruiting shrubs for warm climates.

FIGS

Figs are among the most carefree fruits a home gardener can grow. You can maintain them as bushes or allow them to grow into small trees where winters are very mild. Fig roots can survive temperatures as low as 0°F, but bearing branches are injured by temperatures below 15°F. For this reason, gardeners in the upper South often build plastic-covered shelters to provide winter protection for figs, while fig lovers in the Southwest simply prune off deadwood at winter's end.

Because of the dense shade they provide in the summer, figs have been used in courtyards from New Orleans to San Antonio. Where winters are colder and figs are not likely to grow into trees, they can be used on patios and trained to do espalier tricks. Just be sure that they do not flank entryways, for you don't want to have unsuspecting visitors stepping on fallen fruits and then squashing them around your house.

Figs bear on both old wood and new. Buds that survive winter bear in early summer, and a larger crop appears in fall on the season's new growth. Following harsh winters, expect only the late crop. Prune the trees lightly to shape them and remove dead branches. Figs are ripe when they are large and soft and they lose their green color. Provide water regularly during the second half of the summer, for figs will split if heavy rains follow a long dry spell. Fig fruits are actually fleshy flowers turned inside out.

Figs have enjoyed a recent resurgence in popularity, and many almost-forgotten varieties have been revived and propagated by fig-conscious nurseries. Try two different varieties and experiment with rare finds (see pages 194-195).

In the West, sour fruit beetles sometimes enter figs through the small opening in the fruit called the *eye*. You may be able to avoid damage by choosing varieties with closed ends, such as 'Black Mission' and 'Conadria'.

Once you have a couple of fig trees growing, you can try new varieties by grafting scions onto your trees. This is a hobby in itself, but it's not difficult to learn if you can scare up a local mentor who can demonstrate how it's done.

GRAPES

MUSCADINE GRAPES

These are very easy to grow in the Southeast. Most varieties have thick skins and seeds, and therefore are regarded as less refined than bunch grapes. Yet all muscadines have a distinctive zingy flavor, and the juice is excellent. Muscadine fruits do not grow in dense clusters, like bunch grapes, but do yield many individual grapes in loose clusters — usually more than 25 pounds per mature vine!

Muscadines are much more resistant to diseases than their bunching cousins. They are not bothered by the drenching rains typical of the Southeast, which cause bunch grapes to mildew to death. They must have water, however, and a lack of it causes serious reductions in yield and fruit quality.

A trellis or arbor is required to keep muscadine vines aloft. You may secure them to the posts the first year; after that they will lie over the arbor. Avoid planting them near entryways, as wasps find muscadine arbors to be ideal homes. In many areas, you can visit pick-your-own farms to sample muscadine varieties, and then decide which ones you want to plant. With proper care, muscadines will produce well for decades.

One confusing aspect of muscadines has to do with sex. In muscadine lingo, varieties that do not require the presence of another variety to ensure good pollination are called *male, perfect,* or *self-fruitful.* The others, called *female* or *imperfect,* need a companion male to set fruits, though a single male plant can handle several females. I suppose the perfect/imperfect terminology has been adopted to keep muscadines from of-

---

SCUPPERNONG OR MUSCADINE?

Are scuppernongs and muscadines the same thing? Yes and no. Before there were a hundred varieties to choose from, the popular golden brown muscadine was called a scuppernong, and some people (like my grandmother) called all muscadines scuppernongs. Modern golden-fruited muscadines are but distant relatives of the original scuppernong and are most properly referred to as muscadines.

fending feminine sensibilities, but I for one find it easier to understand in terms of male/female, probably because it is somewhat bizarre.

BUNCH GRAPES

These used to have so many disease problems that growing them without fungicides was impossible in humid areas. But modern varieties from Arkansas ('Reliance' and 'Mars') and Florida ('Orlando Gold') have made them much more resilient and heat hardy. Other American hybrids grown in the West also fit into home landscapes, but choose a variety that can stand up to heat and mildew, such as 'Niabell'. Early-maturing varieties like 'Flame Seedless' can also help grapes escape some damage from the green fruit beetle, which appears in late summer.

All bunch grapes require a sturdy trellis and ruthless pruning. They often grow vigorously enough to provide dense shade when grown on arbors or pergolas, or you can grow them on trellises fashioned from posts and wire.

In winter, prune back the vines until all that's left of the previous year's growth is the main trunk, a couple of arms, and a dozen or so short spurs, or bits of bud-bearing branch. After fruit set in late spring, you may need to remove some of the young clusters so that those that remain will be well supplied with moisture and nutrients. Keep grapes well mulched to reduce their need for supplemental water.

To improve fruit set of bunch grapes, spray the plants with a kelp spray during blossoming. Kelp contains gibberellic acid, which stimulates flowering. More flowers result in heavy, well-filled bunches.

Grapes have many pests, but most of those that attack the leaves, including big sphinx moth larvae, tiny grape leaf rollers, and voracious grape leaf skeletonizers, are easily controlled with Bt-based insecticides. The previously mentioned green fruit beetle appears in late summer in the West, but its eastern counterpart, the Japanese beetle, starts eating grapes as soon as they become sweet and soft. Paper bags fastened around grape clusters will keep either pest at bay.

WINTERIZE YOUR MUSCADINES

When winter temperatures dip below 15°F, muscadines may be killed back to their roots, which seriously cuts the next year's yields. Where winters are cold, try this method of winter protection: After the vines lose their leaves in late fall, free them from their trellis, lay them on the ground, and cover them with straw and a sheet of plastic. After the last spring frost, remove the protective mulch, raise the vines, and tie them to their trellis.

RASPBERRIES

Raspberries are better adapted to cool climates where spring lasts a long time, although some varieties can handle the heat and disease pressure encountered in the Sunbelt when grown in partial shade. Raspberries often become infected with viruses, which cause the plants to decline and the berries to fall apart. I have seen the 'Heritage' variety grown successfully in Zone 9 when given plenty of compost and water. A relatively new cultivar called 'Bababerry' is being tried throughout the Sunbelt, but its reliability in various locations is still being evaluated. Check with your Extension Service agent to see if it has been grown successfully in your area.

Unlike blackberries, which bear only on one-year-old (or biennial) canes, some raspberries can be managed so that they bear a single fall crop on new canes. 'Heritage' and 'Autumn Bliss' are the highest-yielding members of this primocane group. To grow them, mow all canes down to the ground in winter and nurture the new canes that appear in spring. With consistent irrigation, you should be enjoying fresh raspberries in August, after blackberries, blueberries, and most tree fruits are long gone.

Black raspberries, often called blackcaps, need quite a bit of space, since they propagate by sinking the tips of long canes into the soil. These tips then develop into new plants. This "walking" tendency is fine along pasture fencerows, but it can get out of hand in a small yard. Like other raspberries, blackcaps are best adapted to the upper South and mountain areas, but try them anyplace where you can provide water for them throughout the spring and early summer.

STRAWBERRIES

Strawberries are extremely cold-hardy plants. They like acidic soil that's been generously enriched with organic matter and full sun for at least two-thirds of the day. After they bear in the spring, strawberries go through a period of summer dormancy in warm climates. Everbearing strawberries or varieties described as "day neutral" will continue to bear throughout the summer and fall, but you must keep them fed, watered, and partially shaded to get good long-season production. In the West, cover strawberries with shade cloth in midsummer to keep them alive until fall.

Water all strawberries periodically during the summer to keep them alive, but don't expect much growth. Strawberries grow best in cool weather. Beds should be renovated every fall, with only young, healthy plants kept into the next season. If the spring is dry, water strawberries regularly from the time the first blossoms appear until the last fruits are picked.

In the East, where spring rainfall is usually overabundant, many people grow their strawberries in slightly raised rows to keep them from drowning. When the rainy season ends, a mulch helps keep the strawberry bed moist. In many parts of the West, where salty soil and dry conditions prevail, strawberries are grown in shallow trenches between rows. The hills of soil on either side help capture accumulated salts, while most irrigation water seeps into the trenches where it is most needed.

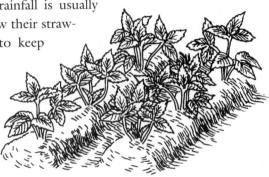

In the East, grow strawberries in raised rows.

Whichever way you plant them, it's crucial that strawberries be set at the proper depth. The central crown should be exposed (never buried) but not sitting high up on top of the soil.

Mulch strawberries with acidic materials such as pine straw or chopped leaves to control weeds and retain soil moisture. Slugs are a formidable strawberry enemy; keep plants spaced

In the West, grow them in shallow trenches.

at least 6 inches apart to discourage them and leave room for traps and barriers. Workable approaches to slug control are outlined in chapter 7 beginning on page 178.

Strawberries can be very versatile when put to work in edible landscapes. They are a natural border plant for informal walkways, and they make great ground covers beneath small trees that don't cast too much shade. Since many varieties literally drip with runners from mid-fall until spring, they work well when allowed to spill over the tops of retaining walls or large containers.

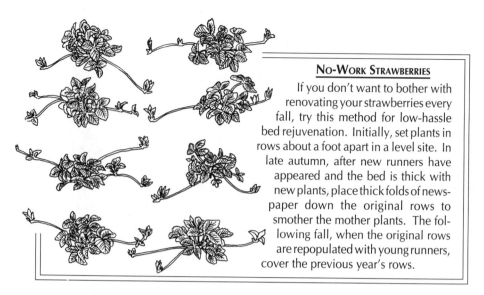

OBSCURE SMALL FRUITS

The following lesser-known small fruits can be valuable landscape plants if you require both taste and beauty of your yard. Many have not been selected as extensively as more popular fruits, and flavor can vary from plant to plant. To find the best keepers, you may want to start out with several, and then thin them back after you know which plants bear the best-tasting fruits. They grow best where the climate and soil are exactly to their liking, so look for special niches that meet their peculiar requirements.

AUTUMN AND RUSSIAN OLIVES

Autumn and Russian olives are members of the *Elaeagnus* genus of nitrogen-fixing shrubs. They are highly ornamental for both flowers and fruits, although fruit flavor varies from plant to plant. Some are sweet enough to eat out of hand; others are better left to the birds. All grow well in partial shade. These shrubs are excellent for hedges and windbreaks in Zones 7 and 8 or for planting among slow-growing hardwood trees.

GOLDEN CURRANTS

The golden currant *(Ribes aureum)*, a western native also known as the buffalo currant, can handle much more heat and drought than other currants, which grow best in cool climates. The fragrant flowers develop into variously colored berries. Fruit flavor also is variable, but these small shrubs are very ornamental. Start out with several plants, then thin them back to the best-tasting ones after they reach bearing age, which usually takes three years. The golden currant is best adapted to the West and may be subject to restrictions in the East due to the roles played by other currants as hosts for white-pine blister rust.

KIWI

Kiwi (*Actinidia* species) develop long, lush twining vines when grown in rich soil, given ample water, and provided with a sturdy arbor or wire trellis. The large-fruited type, *A. chinensis*, is not cold hardy in Zone 7 but may grow very well in parts of Zone 8 and 9 with adequate winter chilling (some varieties require more chilling than others). The smaller-fruited hardy kiwi, *A. arguta*, has comparatively small leaves and fruit but can stand up to prolonged subfreezing temperatures. Within both categories, only a few varieties are self-fertile; usually you will need one male plant for every five or so females.

PINEAPPLE GUAVAS

The pineapple guava *(Feijoa sellowiana)* is a vigorous subtropical shrub from South America and worth trying in Zones 8 and 9. Hard freezes may cause it to lose its leaves, but the plant should survive. For sure fruiting in cold-winter areas, try growing it in containers that can be brought inside during unusually cold weather. Whether in the ground or in containers, mature plants can take heavy pruning, which is often a necessity to keep them from overstepping their bounds.

Both the fleshy flower petals and the fruits of the pineapple guava are edible. Expect the first ripe fruits in early fall. Pineapple guavas are not truly ripe until they drop to the ground, so don't expect great flavor of specimens pulled from the branches.

POMEGRANATES

Pomegranates thrive in alkaline soil. Where soil is acidic, liberally lime the planting site the fall before planting. Pomegranates can take quite a bit of drought once established and even grow well in the desert. You will need to keep them watered while they are holding green fruits, however, because the fruits will split (as tomatoes do) if very wet conditions follow a long dry spell. Where winters are cold, a warm pocket against a south wall is required, for cold hardiness bottoms out at about 15°F. Pomegranates grow into bushes in most locations and are quite ornamental in fall, when they turn bright yellow. 'Wonderful' is the most widely cultivated variety, but several others also are available. Some are grown strictly as ornamentals and bear no fruits.

TREE FRUITS

Many common fruit trees have been grafted onto dwarf rootstocks so that they stay small. It is thus easy to find space for them, and they are easy to prune and spray. Speaking of spraying, some fruit trees are very difficult to grow organically because of chronic problems with various diseases. To improve your chances of success, all deciduous trees (those that drop their leaves in winter) should be sprayed with horticultural oil, available at most garden supply stores, in late winter, before the buds swell. The oil suffocates several common pests that may be hiding on the bark.

During the growing season, you may want to treat your fruit trees to a foliar feeding of kelp and fish emulsion or some other micronutrient spray intended for leaf application. Be sure to offer this foliar banquet on a cloudy day or in early evening, when the hot sun won't cause the water-based spray to burn the leaves.

Fruit trees grown in warm climates are at high risk of being injured by sunscald—a disorder that develops when hot sun heats up chilled or frozen trunks and results in serious damage to the most important part of a tree's anatomy. To protect them from sunscald from the beginning, wrap the trunks of young trees with burlap strips, hardware cloth, or paper wrapping made for this purpose. Later, white latex paint can be substituted for the wrapping. Slap a second coat on the south and west sides of the trunks, where damage is most

DEEP WATERING

When watering fruit trees or bushes, the idea is to soak the soil slowly, so that moisture seeps at least 2 feet down. Always water regularly while the plants are holding green fruits. Use a drip irrigation hose if you have several fruit trees or bushes to water. If you have only a few, try this method: Rake back the mulch and leave it in a raised circle around the trees or bushes. Flood the interior, let the water seep in, and repeat the process two or three times. Replace the mulch.

likely to occur.

The growth of young trees can be seriously retarded by weeds. Keep the area beneath trees free of weeds and Bermuda grass for the first three years. Use mulches rather than cultivation to suppress other weeds, as a surprising portion of a tree's root mass is very close to the surface. When your trees get large enough to claim their own space, undersow them with biennial or perennial clover or another nitrogen-fixing legume.

Almost all tree fruits require thinning to lighten the load on branches and reduce alternate bearing. Following fruit set, many trees will shed part of their load as an attempt at self-thinning (this is called the spring drop). You must complete the job, usually by picking off roughly half of the green

After the X-marked fruit is thinned off, the remaining fruit will grow more vigorously.

NATURAL FUNGICIDES FOR FRUITS

Many fruits, especially grapes, peaches, and nectarines, are very susceptible to many fungal diseases. Chemical fungicides must be constantly reapplied to be effective, and the same goes for organic fungicides. The time to begin a spraying program is *before* a fungus problem develops. Whenever rainstorms come one after another, assume that fungi are having a party in your orchard. The following mixtures often can help prevent serious problems.

Baking soda and water, with a few drops of liquid dishwashing detergent added to help the mixture stick to plant leaves, is gentle, nontoxic, and quite convenient if you have only one or two plants to protect. Use 1 teaspoon per quart of water, and apply with a hand-pump spray bottle.

Lime sulfur is an old standby, long used to kill recently germinated fungus spores and to prevent the proliferation of new ones. The best time to use it is late spring, after the plants have flowered and the last traces of horticultural oil (used in winter) have disappeared. Timing is very important, as the mixture can damage young leaves. Use it after a rainy period (when fungi are likely to be reproducing) and only in the early evening.

Bordeaux mixture has been used for hundreds of years to control foliar diseases of fruit trees and bushes. A mixture of copper sulfate and hydrated lime, it works like a combination of the previous two sprays. Bordeaux is very strong and should always be diluted according to package directions (or even more). If you are going to use bordeaux, use it right: once when flowering begins and again a month later.

Liquid copper is another old remedy for fungal and bacterial diseases. It is somewhat tricky to use, as trees will absorb too much if you let them. Use copper (or copper sulfate) products according to package directions early in the morning so the leaves will dry off quickly.

fruits that remain. In years of light fruit set, no thinning may be needed, but it's always better to thin green fruits than to have to take out entire branches later on, after they break. When you thin hard and early, the payback is larger fruits, healthier trees, and few, if any, broken limbs.

The following trees are worthy of trial in warm-climate gardens. Rather than listing them alphabetically, I've arranged them according to ease of culture and adaptability. The first five (persimmons, pears, plums, and the citrus fruits) can often be grown organically, provided they are planted in hospitable sites. Beyond these five, pay close attention to the various microclimates that your yard has to offer — and to how much time and effort you are willing to devote to tree upkeep.

PERSIMMONS

If you have room for only one or two fruit-bearing trees, consider Oriental, or kaki, persimmons. Cultivars are available for every possible warm-climate growing situation, and persimmon trees have very few problems with pests and diseases. They are also somewhat small as trees go, topping out at about 15 feet when kept pruned. The leaves are dark and glossy, and most varieties are self-fertile. With astringent varieties, wait to eat them until the fruits are fully ripe and have begun to soften.

PEARS

Many pears grow well in warm climates, but not the buttery-tasting types grown in Washington. Instead, we do better with "sand" pears, which stay hard until they start to rot, or various Asian cultivars that are highly resistant to fire blight. (The gritty taste comes from stone cells under the pears' skin. Deep peeling or cooking gets rid of them.) Asian pear trees, sometimes called apple pears, are quite large, growing to 30 feet, and you will need two trees (the second one can be non-Asian) for good pollination. At least one major fruit tree retailer, Stark Brothers, has begun to offer Asian pears in dwarf form. 'Keiffer', the most common pear grown in the Southeast, has Asian pear in its pedigree.

POACHED PEARS

To improve the texture of hard-fleshed pears, poach them in flavored syrup, then chill them before eating. Concoct a light syrup from 1 cup water and 1 cup sugar (more or less). Add 1 teaspoon vanilla, almond, lemon, or some other aromatic extract. Add peeled, chopped pears and simmer until tender. Chill in the syrup and enjoy.

PLUMS

Plums are probably the easiest stone

fruits to grow. They are more disease tolerant than peaches and nectarines and have lower chill requirements than cherries. They also mature early, which makes it possible to grow some varieties in the desert Southwest, where there is but a brief window between the last frost and the emergence of green fruit beetles (the western counterpart of Japanese beetles).

Many varieties are available on dwarf and semidwarf rootstocks. If you do well with plums, branch out into peaches and nectarines. With all the stone fruits, a fungal disease called brown rot is a constant threat. Unless you are willing to follow an intensive fungicide spraying schedule, expect some brown rot. Clean up every affected fruit as soon as you see the first signs of this disease's dreaded brown fuzz.

CITRUS FRUITS

Citrus fruits are wonderful in places where they won't lose their almost-ripe fruits to hard freezes in midwinter. If other people in your area grow citrus trees, so can you. Choose a warm, sheltered location for citrus trees. Good soil drainage and reasonable fertility are needed, but citrus trees generally are not heavy feeders. Too much nitrogen fertilizer can lead to very thick rinds, so use a light hand when feeding these trees.

Citrus pests are seldom serious threats in home gardens. Experiment with many varieties ignored by commercial growers because they are too delicate to ship. Ask around to get information about local favorites before deciding which types of trees to grow. Dwarf trees of many varieties are readily available.

Getting trees on the right types of rootstock for your area should not be much of a problem, since citrus trees for the nursery trade are usually grown locally. In the citrus states of Florida, Arizona, and California, tight shipping restrictions apply to citrus trees to prevent the spread of various pests and diseases. If you live where citrus trees are not generally grown and are marginally hardy, you can order many types of trees through the mail. Sour orange or mandarin orange rootstock is generally more winter hardy than sweet orange stock. In addition, rare-fruit nurseries often stock unusual Oriental cultivars that are more cold hardy than the types of citrus sold in supermarkets.

KUMQUATS

Kumquats are close relatives of citrus fruits, and nurseries sometimes graft them onto sour orange rootstock. Properly listed as genus *Fortunella*, kumquats are the most winter hardy of the citrus family, and also the only form of citrus fruit with a sweet, edible rind. A long, warm summer is required for good fruit production, but the plants themselves have no trouble with a few hard freezes every winter.

Besides being valued for their fruits, kumquats make good landscape plants, since they are small, rarely growing more than 10 feet tall, and have dense, dark evergreen leaves. Kumquats are orange in color and flavor and may be round or oval in shape. They have been successfully crossed with limes to create a novel fruit called the limequat, which makes a good substitute for limes where winters are too cold for true citrus trees.

Where winters are quite cold but summers are long, either kumquats or limequats may be grown in large containers and brought indoors during the coldest months. When handled properly, these container-grown 'quats are more likely to fruit indoors than other types of citrus trees.

HEALTH WATCH FOR FRUIT ROOTS

Texas root rot is a fungus that frequently infests alkaline soils that are low in organic matter. Many plants are susceptible to having their roots stripped by this disease. Except for citrus trees, fruit trees tend to be easy victims. Stricken plants wilt rather suddenly in midsummer, never to recover. If Texas root rot is known to be present in your area and you have high-risk soil, use plenty of organic matter when preparing planting holes for long-lived fruits. Also adjust the pH with preplanting applications of soil sulfur and ammonium sulfate.

APPLES

The likelihood that you will harvest beautiful, delicious apples from any apple tree grown organically south of Zone 7 is very low. The best apple varieties require more winter chilling than is available in most warm climates, although a few, including 'Ana' and 'Adina', will bear where winters are mild. If your Extension Service does suggest any apple cultivars for your area, pay very close attention to training and pruning when you try out those trees. As long as the trees are trained and the fruits are thinned, a well-adapted cultivar stands a good chance of bearing every year, since apples bloom late. Diseases and insects may mar some of the fruits, but the damage usually is cosmetic and of little concern if your main interest is eating apples, not selling them. Crab apples are more widely adaptable, more resistant to disease, and in all ways easier to grow.

PEACHES

Over the years, I have received several heartbreaking letters from gardeners whose peach trees refused to fruit, got sick, or mysteriously died three years after they were planted. If the truth be told, peaches are subject to all sorts of problems, although there are always exceptional situations where you hit the right combination of cultivar and site and get good peaches every year.

To improve your chances of success, choose varieties recommended by your Extension Service (they'll best fit your climate's chill hours). Purchase them in dwarf or semidwarf form to make it easy to keep them meticulously clean. In winter, after you have cleaned up every fallen leaf and fruit, carefully inspect the bark for evidence of various pests and attack them with your hands or a stiff brush. Yearly pruning of peaches is mandatory, for trees splinter easily when they become unbalanced or loaded with fruits. A midwinter application of horticultural oil should be the final touch after pruning.

In the spring, peaches often lose their fruits to freezes that occur while the trees are still in flower. Be prepared to cover the blossoming trees with old blankets on cold nights to reduce frost damage. Commercial orchardists often mist their trees with water on cold nights, which protects some blossoms from damage with a thin coat of ice.

Finally, always thin back green fruits in years of heavy fruit set. Left unattended, peach trees will literally die of neglect.

CHERRIES

The problem with cherries is that they require more winter chilling than is available in most warm climates. This is especially true of sweet cherries. If you are determined to try cherries, go with a tart cherry such as 'North Star'. Cherries are subject to the same diseases as plums and peaches, and they may mysteriously drop all their fruits following periods of very wet or very dry weather. Cherries can surprise you, though, by bearing heavy crops of delicious fruits, and they are certainly worth a try in Zone 7 in the East and in mountain areas in the West where winters are cold.

APRICOTS

Apricots are beautiful ornamental trees, but it is very difficult to get fruits from them unless you live where spring frosts end very early. Apricots bloom very early in the spring — and often are promptly damaged by late frosts. Later on, the fruits often become infected with the same brown rot that bothers other stone fruits.

If you are determined to try an apricot tree (most are self-fertile), purchase a dwarf to make maintenance and frost protection easier. Plant it where you can enjoy the fragrant spring blossoms, since beautiful flowers may be all you will ever get unless you live in a warm, semi-arid location.

CONCLUSION

Rather than end on a negative note, let me reemphasize how rewarding it can be to find the biggest blackberries you've ever seen 20 feet from your back door and to experience the wonderful feeling of biting into a soft, really ripe fig. By aligning your hopes and dreams with the most promising fruit species, you can surely grow several excellent fruits with ease. So what if you can't grow everything that thrives in Oregon or New Jersey! The important thing is to do a good job of growing what fruits you can. If you ask around and take chances with unusual fruits, you are sure to find a few that like your home as much as you do.

Chapter Five

FUNDAMENTAL FLOWERS

BEAUTIFUL, FRAGRANT, AND FUN TO GROW, flowers are easy to appreciate and hard to resist. But for flowers to be truly useful, they should do more than just look good. To me, a really good flower will make perfume I can smell, shade a hot spot on the deck, or attract life forms I enjoy, like butterflies, hummingbirds, or parasitic wasps. Many of my favorite flowers also can be cut and brought indoors.

For a long time, I was so preoccupied with food plants that I missed the fun of growing flowers. There are literally hundreds of species to discover, and it's easy to get lost in them. Every year, I find myself strangely obsessed with some little-known flower, and I must work with it until I have learned its talents and drawbacks. This happens to a lot of gardeners, and it can be both a wonder and a curse. Although there is nothing wrong with becoming passionately involved with any one species, such as roses or daylilies, it's important not to neglect the many other flowers that can bring a smile to your face and beauty to your yard.

Because of the excitement flowers somehow manage to impart, it pays to start out on a rational note, getting organized and setting priorities. I've put together six general goals to help keep your flowering aspirations intact. After briefly reviewing these strategies for happy flowering, I'll look at the best bloomers for warm climates, including perennials, bulbs, vines, biennials, and annuals.

* **Seek out and study adapted perennials and perpetual bulbs.** Although they will occupy a relatively small amount of space, they will provide rich accents and continuity from year to year. The best ones require very little maintenance.

* **Use shade-giving vines.** What better way to keep a brick wall from heating up or to shade a window that gets too much sun than to cover it with dripping tendrils or delicate flowers during the hottest months of the year?

* **Use hardy annuals and biennials.** Fall to winter flowers are fun to work with and very rewarding.

* **Experiment with annual combinations.** Bedding flowers can help unify perennials, cover for fading bulbs and biennials, and provide color accents. Many are very easy to grow from purchased plants or seeds.

* **Incorporate filler flowers.** White flowers or plants with grayish foliage can tie together eclectic beds and all sorts of plant groupings.

* **Fill window boxes and containers.** Since these flowers are viewed up close, they are among the most valuable. Many plants grown in beds in cool climates do best in containers in warm climates.

Now let's look at each of these subjects in depth and incorporate some tried-and-true tricks of garden design.

THE ELEMENT OF DESIGN

Matching plants to appropriate sites is among a gardener's greatest challenges. Not far behind is the element of design, which can be delightful or disastrous. Unless you have a clear vision of how shrubs, trees, and flowers will work together to enhance your home and its views, consult a good book or get professional help.

If you design your own landscape, put some thought into it. Consult reference books at your local library to get information about basic dos and don'ts. Look for *The Complete Home Landscape Designer* by Joel M. Lerner, *Easy Garden Design* by Janet Macunovich, and other books that seem tailor-made for do-it-yourselfers. (See Chapter 8.) Also look at other yards in your area, as well as botanical gardens, and make note of the trees, shrubs, flowers, and plant combinations you find particularly attractive.

Once you have a drawing in hand, you don't have to follow it exactly. However, do follow your plan when it comes to scale or the size of the plants recommended. If you make substitutions, try to stick with like species. For example, you might choose a dwarf peach or plum in place of an ornamental cherry tree, or a fruiting pomegranate in place of one prized mostly for its flowers.

With some type of scheme in place for existing shrubs, trees, and other features, and some plan for desired edibles, get started having fun with flowers, grasses, and ground covers. As you dive into the wonderful sea of landscape design, understanding the following phrases will be helpful.

Foundation plants are large and small shrubs and trees used to structure the design. Foundation plants also serve as a visual buffer between house and not house. Most are evergreen and look good in winter, when the rest of the yard may appear quite dead. Select very well-adapted foundation plants that require little care. If not dwarf in habit, they may need pruning at least once a year. Check local nurseries for hollies, azaleas, boxwoods, photinias (redtips), nandinas, yews, and other foundation shrubs well suited to your area.

Do You Need Professional Help?

The best way to find a designer is through his or her work. If you know of a yard or commercial landscape that you really like, ask who designed it. Commercial landscapes often are the most up-to-date in terms of reduced maintenance and water requirements and use of quality plant materials.

If you are working with a professional designer, decide from the beginning how much of the plant purchasing and planting you want to do yourself. Design services cost less when the designer works for a business that will profit from installing your landscape. If a design is all you want, make that clear from the outset and expect to pay for this professional service. You can ask for only a front-yard or entryway design and keep the backyard as your own personal project.

Foundation plants serve as a buffer between house and nonhouse.

Specimen plant

Mass planting

Border

Specimen plants are so large and exciting that one to three of them is all it takes to create substantial visual interest. Roses and other fragrant flowering bushes often are used as specimens, as is pampas grass. Specimens also can be placed within borders as focus points (like visual punctuation marks). Beware! A landscape with many lone specimens but little in the way of foundation or borders seems disjointed. If collecting is in your blood, let stone and stucco work in combination with specimen plants to create special effects.

Mass plantings are the opposite of specimens. More than twenty plants set out together so that they form a swath of like foliage and flowers qualify as a mass planting. If you fall in love with a flower that loves you back, try massing it for the most exciting visual sensation a gardener is likely to experience.

A **border** is like a picture frame for a section of the landscape. It usually has more than one layer of plants, which creates depth. An informal border may include many different plants, grouped together in clumps or drifts, that come into bloom at different times of year. In a formal border, plant combinations are either repeated over and over or are laid out in uniform lines (as in hedges or evergreens with color flowers in the foreground).

An **edging** is less than a border and more like a lining for fixed features such as sidewalks, driveways, or larger flower beds. Edgings usually comprise a single, low-growing plant such as alyssum, candytuft, strawberries, mondo grass, or dwarf annual flowers such as French marigolds.

PERENNIALS

Perennial flowers are useful throughout the landscape, since they come back year after year and the best-adapted ones become more robust with age. Perennials may be used as specimens, in mass plantings, or in smaller border drifts. A few, such as small sedums and candytuft, make good edging material.

Many people tell beginning gardeners to stay away from perennials because so many of them fail in warm climates. I think that's poor advice. Since perennials are the flowers you'll keep for many years, as cornerstones of mood and color, try the best ones first, one at a time.

Another reason not to hold back when planning places for perennials is that these plants are what horticulturists call *site specific*. In other words, they have rather exact requirements about exposure, soil moisture, companions, and so forth. Since they lack flexibility in what they expect from the world, you have to put them only where they like to be.

On the plus side, part of the beauty of growing perennials is when you do it. Much of the work — sowing, propagating, and transplanting — goes on in fall and winter. When you work with perennials, the growing season never ends.

Envision most perennials as companionable accent plants that will be surrounded by annuals, biennials, shrubs, and ornamental grasses. Here are some other guidelines for warm-climate gardeners with perennials on their minds:

* Never judge a perennial in its first year, unless it's dead. After the second year, propagate or be prepared for the plant to perish.

* When choosing perennials, lean toward wildflowers, their close relatives, and local favorites.

* Even drought-tolerant species require water their first year to help them get established.

* Start with a few species and expand as you learn. With perennials, every new species is an adventure.

* Pay close attention to microclimate when choosing planting sites. Proper drainage, air circulation, sun exposure, and soil

---

DROUGHT-RESISTANT PERENNIALS

In sites where it will be difficult to water, look for these characteristics among perennial flowers:

* Plants with small, thick leaves (cacti and sedums)
* Plants whose natural period of dormancy is midsummer (columbines and spider lilies)
* Plants that form stolons or tubers, as opposed to fibrous roots (butterfly weed and daylilies)
* Plants normally seen on roadsides (goldenrod and black-eyed Susans)

---

pH often are crucial.

❋ Seek out single-flower varieties and species. They usually bloom longer and don't require as much deadheading to keep them pretty.

PROPAGATING PERENNIALS

Most perennials grow in clumps. One of the secrets of growing clump-forming perennials in warm climates is to propagate new plants every fall, even if books tell you they must be divided only every three years. It is not always necessary to dig up the parent plant and divide it. Instead, propagate basal rosettes and stems or take plantlets off the outside of the clump. In so doing, you can easily multiply plants so that a lone clump turns into three in the course of one winter. Here's how you do it:

In early fall, look for low stems that hug the ground on plants such as

dianthus, mint, monarda, and candytuft. Cut them from the parent plant and place them in containers or a nursery bed. When new roots have developed, transplant them to where you want them to grow.

Cut the small plantlet off the mother plant and replant it.

On plants with big crowns, such as Shasta daisies and coreopsis, remove clustered rosettes of leaves where they emerge from the main stem in mid-autumn. Plant them 1 inch deep in containers or a nursery bed and keep them moist. Transplant them when new roots develop.

With plants that form dense clumps (daylilies, yarrow, and irises), dig the clump, separate the plants, and replant them in mid-fall every other year. The divided plants will be healthier and will bloom more than if they were left undivided.

For daylilies, dig the entire clump and then separate it into new plants.

Here are some perennials that are promising candidates for

warm-climate gardens, though they are but a few of the hundreds of excellent perennials now in propagation. Most are widely available from garden centers and mail-order nurseries.

TWENTY PRIME PERENNIALS

BEE BALM (MONARDA DIDYMA)

Types: Cultivated forms are refined versions of a native American mint. Monarda grows best in partial shade with supplemental water. Long, hot summers can cause them to be short-lived, but new plants are always popping up to replace the old ones. Wild-looking blossoms attract bees and humming-birds.

Seasons: Bloom time is midsummer. Plant seeds in fall or very early spring; set out transplants before the weather gets hot. Or, you can propagate by taking rooted sprigs from the outside of the clump in early spring. You may also root plants from cuttings taken in summer.

Tips:

* Drought-tolerant only in late summer.

* Locate monarda where you can easily view the insects and hummingbirds that visit the flowers.

BLUE FLAX (LINUM PERENNE LEWISII)

Types: Especially in arid climates, these plants cool off hot pockets with their grayish foliage and blue flowers, which come and go daily all summer.

Seasons: In the fall or early spring, direct-seed where you want them to grow. When transplanting container-grown plants, keep the root ball intact.

Tips:

* Water periodically to encourage reblooming.

* Blue flax benefits from a booster feeding with manure tea or another liquid fertilizer in midsummer.

BUTTERFLY WEED (ASCLEPIAS SPECIES)

Types: This native American flower has recently been hybridized, but the choice species remains *A. tuberosa*.

Seasons: Plant in early spring or fall. When working with seeds, fall planting is preferred. Unless you are a patient and experienced seed starter, shop for plants at a reputable nursery. Buy only nursery-propagated plants.

Tips:

* Transplant carefully and be gentle with the thick main root. Plants need two years to reach mature size.

* Extreme tolerance of drought, heat, and cold make this flower a top choice.

CACTUS (CACTACEAE FAMILY, INCLUDING *CACTI* SPECIES)

Types: Hundreds are indigenous to the Southwest, and many make nice specimen plants. Prickly pear types can tolerate the moisture typical of the Southeast. All cacti require full sun and resent heavy watering. Mulch them with decorative stones.

Seasons: Propagate in spring by placing the scar ends of individual "leaves" in sandy soil. Do not water for at least a month. Feed cacti at least once a year, in early summer.

Tips:

* Locate where children will not be tempted to play with the spines but the nocturnal blossoms can be seen and enjoyed after dark.

CANDYTUFT *(IBERIS* SPECIES*)*

Types: Perennial candytuft, *I. sempervirens,* is evergreen in warm climates and benefits from a little shade. Although not particularly showy on its own, it makes a versatile partner for bulbs and shrubs that bloom in spring.

Seasons: Plant seeds or purchased plants in fall or spring. Root cuttings in summer and set them out in fall.

Tips:

* Interplant candytuft with daffodils or other bulbs, or use it between azaleas or roses.

* Keep a few plants on hand for spicing up container assortments.

COLUMBINE (*AQUILEGIA* SPECIES)

Types: Timeless favorites for shade that make long-lasting cut flowers and often reseed. Predominant colors are yellow and rust-red, although *A. coerulea* (Rocky Mountain columbine) is dependably blue and white. In late winter and spring, when they are actively growing, all columbines need a lot of moisture.
Seasons: Rarely flower the first year from seeds. Start seeds in the fall or late winter. Bloom time is late spring. Foliage deteriorates after flowering, and plants are semidormant throughout the summer.

Tips:

* Allow to grow undisturbed in a shady spot on the north side of your house, where other flowers will not grow.

COREOPSIS (*COREOPSIS* SPECIES)

Types: Perhaps the best perennial for beginners, these bright yellow flowers of early summer thrive on neglect. Tall, lance-leafed wildings dug from ditches are fine, or you can experiment with a number of refined cultivars, including 'Moonbeam.' An annual coreopsis, calliopsis, is also a good bet. Both annual and perennial forms deserve a try in wildflower meadows.
Seasons: If you sow seeds in fall, they will bloom the following spring. Or, take leafy rosettes from mature plants in early fall and set them in containers or a nursery bed until they develop roots. Mature clumps are self-perpetuating, even when mowed down in late summer.

Tips:

* Ideal companion for Shasta daisies.

* Coreopsis grows well on slopes and in dry, rocky places where most cultivated flowers will not grow.

DAHLIA (*DAHLIA* SPECIES)

Types: Extensive hybridization has led to various categories based on flower type. Varieties that grow 3 to 4 feet high produce dramatic cut flowers on stately bushes (they must be securely staked). Dwarf dahlias quickly fill vacancies in any sunny flower bed.
Seasons: Set out tubers in early spring. When working with seeds, sow them

indoors in late winter and set them out in spring. In places where the soil freezes 4 inches deep, lift the roots in fall and store them in a cool place through the winter.

Tips:

* Place three dahlias of the same color and form together for wonderful dramatic effect.

* Except for dwarf strains, all dahlias need serious staking.

* Enrich the soil with compost prior to planting and mulch in early summer to retain moisture.

DAYLILY (*HEMEROCALLIS* SPECIES)

Types: Avoid the old, orange daylilies that grow wild on roadsides, for newer varieties are just as vigorous and much more free-flowering. A mass of like-colored daylilies provides beautiful erosion control on steep banks. The flowering period varies with the variety; some of the newer ones rebloom all summer. Many varieties are evergreen in warm climates. All daylilies are very dependable and easy to grow.

Seasons: Plant anytime except midsummer. Fall and spring are the best times to dig and divide crowded clumps. Daylilies are not picky about soil as long as they have at least half a day of full sun.

Tips:

* Provide water if necessary in late spring and early summer, while daylilies are in flower.

* Irises make fine bed partners for daylilies.

* Dwarf varieties may be grown in containers; try combining them with petunias or other trailing annuals.

FIREWHEEL, BLANKETFLOWER (*GAILLARDIA* SPECIES)

Types: Easy to grow and drought resistant, these native yellow and red flowers can handle full sun. A dwarf form, 'Goblin,' grows to only 12 inches, but expect 30-inch plants when purchasing by species (*G. grandiflora* or *G. aristata*). The annual form, *G. pulchella*, also is easy and dependable.

Seasons: Start seeds in early fall or late winter. Take divisions from established clumps in late winter.

Tips:

  * An excellent companion for coreopsis, marigolds, or yellow zinnias.

FOUR-O'CLOCK *(MIRABILIS SPECIES)*

Types: Look for these classic flowers as *M. jalapa* (the cultivated strain, which includes the bicolored 'Jingles' variety) or *M. multiflora*, a magenta species native to the Southwest.

Seasons: Plant seeds in winter, as chilling improves germination. Plants grow slowly at first but become shrubs by midsummer. Move tuberous roots in the winter when the plants are dormant.

Tips:

  * These are dependable perennials in warm climates, but you can reseed them like an annual.

  * Locate in places you frequent in the afternoon and evening, when the flowers are open.

GAY-FEATHER, BLAZING-STAR *(LIATRIS SPECIES)*

Types: The striking spikes are eye-catching during the second half of summer in both flower beds and cut arrangements. These flowers grow wild on stream banks, and thus they're most at home in moist, well-drained soil in less than full sun.

Seasons: Seeds are difficult to sprout, but you can try them in late winter. Plant divisions or nursery-propagated plants in early spring.

Tips:

  * Mature plants have long taproots that make them very difficult to move.

  * Grow liatris in clusters for the best natural effect.

MAIDEN PINK *(DIANTHUS DELTOIDES)*

Types: Annual dianthus need a lot of water and cool weather, but not the perennial form, *D. deltoides*. Pink, red, and mixed colors are available; all are less than a foot high. After flowering begins to sputter in early summer, shear them back to induce matting and encourage fall reblooming.

Seasons: Seeds sown in fall will bloom their first spring. Container-grown seedlings may be set out all winter if covered for a few weeks with milk jug cloches. You can also start seeds in late winter.

Tips:

* During the first year or two, when the ground cover is sparse and easily invaded by weeds, oversow lightly with toadflax *(Linaria)*, a tiny summer annual.

PENSTEMON *(PENSTEMON* SPECIES*)*

Types: Numerous forms grow wild in the West. They require a replication of their natural habitat to grow well in a garden. Among the showiest, most adaptable species are *P. gentianoides* (large flower spikes bearing tubular flowers in shades of pink) and *P. barbatus* (tall, red spikes).

Seasons: Sow seeds in fall or early spring. Set out purchased plants in early spring.

Tips:

* These diverse flowers are best adapted to dry climates, so water sparingly.

* In wet, humid climates, grow in containers with excellent drainage.

PURPLE CONEFLOWER *(ECHINACEA PURPUREA)*

Types: More regal and refined than other wildflowers, *E. purpurea* also requires good soil. If the site is rich, well drained, and sunny, a clump will persist for many years.

Seasons: Sow seeds in early fall or take divisions in late winter. Buy nursery-grown plants in early spring.

Tips:

* Add lime to acidic soils, as this flower likes a nearly neutral pH.

RUDBECKIA (*RUDBECKIA* SPECIES)

Types: This huge family includes black-eyed Susans, yellow coneflowers, and an assortment of yellow daisies. All will grow in full sun, but they flower best with a little afternoon shade.

Seasons: Plant seeds in late summer in flats or where you want them to grow. Set out purchased plants in fall. Some strains may need frequent replanting unless flowers are allowed to develop mature seeds and reseed themselves.

Tips:

✳ Strains that produce double flowers lack grace; avoid them.

✳ Some selections prefer to be grown as biennials, while others are very long-lived.

✳ This whole tribe tends to fall over after midsummer rainstorms, just when the flowers are reaching their peak. One easy way to stake them is to cover the planting with an arch of rabbit fencing when the plants are about a

Rudbeckia staked with an arch of fencing

foot tall. The plants will then grow through the wire and quickly hide it with new foliage.

SEDUM (*SEDUM* SPECIES)

Types: Low-growing species such as *S. acre* and *S. spurium* may be used as ground covers in dry areas, especially near stone walkways. *S. spectabile*, or autumn-flowering sedum, grows to 18 inches tall and does well in partial shade.
Seasons: Divide plants in the spring. Sedums are very easy to propagate, and they grow new roots willingly.

Tips:

* Sedums are often planted around the trunks of hardwood trees, such as oaks.

* All sedums are wonderful to use around rocks and stones.

SHASTA DAISY (*CHRYSANTHEMUM SUPERBUM*)

Types: Dependable perennials in Zones 7 and 8, but farther South, grow them as hardy annuals. Varieties vary in terms of height, stiffness of stem, and longevity. Experiment with several varieties. Shastas bred for florists' use are not as robust as some others. I like 'May Queen', which is very similar to the oxeye daisy, a naturalized wildflower. All Shasta daisies make long-lasting cut flowers.
Seasons: Plant in the fall for spring bloom. Divide clumps in the fall at least every other year.

Tips:

* If Shasta daisies grow too vigorously in a cultivated bed, move them to a more remote location and use them for cutting.

* The low evergreen growth serves as a nice ground cover in winter.

VERBENA (*VERBENA* SPECIES)

Types: Several species and hybrids have versatile uses, including *V. peruviana* for containers and flowering ground covers, *V. rigida* for difficult slopes, and *V. pulchella* for hanging baskets. All tolerate drought well once they are established.

Seasons: Start seeds in the fall or buy plants early in the spring. Some of the best strains are vegetatively propagated and must be purchased as plants.

Tips:

* Start with a local favorite known to be well adapted to your climate.

Yarrow (Achillea species)

Types: Many species have made their way into warm-climate gardens. The most common ones are *A. filipendulina*, with large, flat clusters of yellow flowers on stiff stems, and *A. millefolium* and its hybrids, in soft pastel colors. Rose and soft yellow dominate most seed mixtures.

Seasons: Plant seeds in late winter indoors and set out the plants in the spring. Transplant the many babies produced by mature plants in the spring or fall, whenever rain is expected.

Tips:

* Plan to water the first year. After that, drought tolerance is excellent.

* Achilleas can become weedy and invasive, so keep an eye on them. Great for slopes, ditches, and wildflower meadows.

Wild about Wildflowers

Wildflower seed mixtures that promise to cover bare ground with a riotous mixture of beautiful flowers sound too good to be true — and they are. You may get a small assortment of flowers blooming the first year, but after that, weeds and grasses will likely outcompete the flowers that somehow managed to germinate in the first place.

Still, there are ways to create and maintain a wildflower meadow. Start with a few wildflowers recommended for your area. The National Wildflower Resource Center (the address and more information is given on page 196 can get you started choosing the best species.

Once you have identified a few species that seem appropriate for the site you have in mind, get started on a two-pronged planting approach. Direct-sow some seeds and start others in flats to rear as transplants. Meanwhile, purchase perennial plants that are difficult to start from seeds and plant them out (the

Wildflower Resource Center can refer you to reliable local sources for nursery-propagated plants).

With a foundation of native wildflowers under way, consider enriching your site with color flowers — nonnative annual and biennial flowers that look like wildflowers even though they are not. Poppies, sweet William, most daisies, toadflax, and many other flowers fit into this category. In contrast, petunias and other bedding plants don't look like wildflowers and appear predictably awkward if you plant them among sprightly, single-flowered wildings.

You can stud the wildflower meadow with divisions from perennials grown in flower beds, including yarrow, coreopsis, and stiff verbena. In fact, propagating perennials and plugging them into the meadow will be rather intense for more than a year as your site is maturing.

In warm climates, wildflower meadows are usually mowed down in late summer or early fall, depending on the importance of late-blooming species such as goldenrod and Joe-Pye weed. For reseeding purposes, seed-bearing "hay" from various wildflowers can be piled where you want more plants to appear.

The best time to use a wildflower seed mixture is after several species have been established in the site. When used this way, the mixtures can help you discover new species that find the site to their liking.

One last note on wildflowers: Avoid planting them where fescue or other cool-season grasses predominate. These grasses easily outcompete many wildflowers, especially those that grow at least a little during the winter months. On the other hand, ornamental oats and wheat and other annual grasses, used sparingly, can enhance the visual drama of wind as it passes through the wildflower meadow. Perennial ornamental grasses that grow in tight clumps are also nice touches.

Vines for Shade and Beauty

Vines are an integral part of the natural ecology of many warm climates. In arid places, they often are a mark of human habitation, but wherever moist pockets of soil occur at the edges of woodlands, you are likely to find vines. Wild vines such as Virginia creeper and trumpet vine can be put to work in home landscapes, but many other choices are available. Local nurseries are often the best places to find vines that show superior local adaptation.

With few exceptions, vines like to have their root area shaded or well mulched, then lift their heads into the sun. When planting vines, incorporate lots of moisture-holding organic matter into the site and make plans for a trellis. A few vines (such as creeping fig and English ivy) will hold on to a wall with suckerlike roots, but most need the support of a fence or trellis.

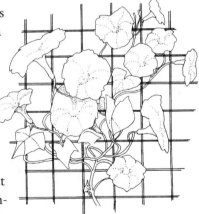

Most vines are rampant growers that must be kept in check through pruning. Before you plant a perennial vine, make a commitment to keep it shaped and confined to where you want it to grow. If you inherit a vine that is wildly out of hand, cut it off at ground level in early spring and start early training the new growth when it appears. Don't be surprised if some of that new growth appears in unlikely places as the vine attempts to regenerate itself by developing stems on roots some distance from its former trunk.

Some vines cling and climb with weaving stems.

Once you get used to having a vine somewhere, you will really miss it if it's gone. For permanence, look for perennial species that become woody over

time, even though they must be pruned at least yearly. Following are the three easiest ones to grow that offer fragrance along with vining demeanor:

*   **Akebia** — fragrant purple flowers and fruits

*   **Jasmine** — many species, most of them yellow and fragrant

*   **Wisteria** — very fragrant purple or white flowers

All three of these should be purchased from a reputable nursery. There are many variations among cultivars, so before you make your choice, study selections carefully and talk with local nursery people if you can. Otherwise, use the free information service offered by better mail-order nurseries.

Beans attach with coiling tendrils.

In tropical areas, many other vine-growing adventures are possible. Most tropical vines are best adapted to partial shade, as they are most at home colonizing trees in rain forest–like situations. The following three vines are easy and rewarding, although they do require humusy soil and supplemental water:

*   **Allamanda** — easy to train over posts or stumps; large, yellow, fragrant flowers

*   **Lapageria** (Chilean bellflower) — clusters of buttery yellow flowers

*   **Mandevilla** — needs a sturdy trellis for its evergreen foliage and beautiful pink flowers

Other vines climb with twining leaf stalks.

A BONANZA OF BULBS

Bulbs are special, fat-footed perennials that store nutrients in bulbous underground parts. True bulbs resemble onions inside and include daffodils, tulips, and most lilies. Many other plants that store energy in thick roots (dahlia and calla lily), rhizomes (iris), or circular corms (gladiolus and caladium) are often thought of as bulbs.

All of these plants have periods of active growth and flowering; most then grow for a while before going dormant. The hardest part of growing bulbs is resisting the temptation to trim back the tops after the flowers fade. This is a big-time no-no, for bulbs use the postblooming period to manufacture energy for next year's flowers.

With thoughtful planning, you may be able to hide (or at least camouflage) bulb foliage with other plants. For example, when early-flowering daffodils and summer-flowering daylilies are grown together, the daylily foliage covers the daffodil leaves quite nicely. Hardy annuals and biennials (which are discussed in the next section) also make nice covers for spring bulbs, since these flower at about the same time the spring bulb foliage die. When bulb foliage begins to turn yellow (or gets badly infested with aphids or other insects), cut it off near the ground and compost it. Don't pull, or the bulb may come up, too.

Most bulbs are perpetual in warm climates, meaning they come back year after year when given minimal care. A few, however, must be dug up and stored in boxes or bags while they are dormant. The reasons vary with location. Tulip bulbs left in the ground in the West may get eaten by gophers and mice. Near the Gulf Coast, they will not get sufficient winter chilling to promote good bloom and may rot from excessive soil moisture. Where winters are cold, there is no need to dig them up.

When working with any bulb, find out what the local customs are and handle bulbs the way experienced gardeners do. Then experiment. I discovered that there's really no need to dig and store gladiolus in my climate, although many gardeners do. Caladium corms, however, quickly turn to mush after a minor hard freeze.

When deciding where to plant bulbs, don't think in straight lines. The lush flowers look best when they arise from a clump of foliage. Plant formal flower bed bulbs such as lilies and amaryllis in clusters of three to five bulbs. If you are striving for a naturalized look with daffodils, crocuses, or scillas, plant them in drifts or islands, not stiff geometric shapes.

Unless you are planting a bunch of bulbs close together and plan to excavate and refill the site, buy a bulb planter. This inexpensive hand tool eliminates laborious digging by pulling out bulb-sized plugs of soil. Then, you simply drop the bulbs into the holes.

All bulbs like to find a bit of food stashed under their roots. Bonemeal is the old standby, but many bulb lovers enthusiastically endorse the use of special bulb fertilizers, since they deliver more nutrients than bonemeal alone. The important thing is to put the fertilizer under the bulb when you plant it. Later, fertilize bulbs from the soil's surface after the blooms have faded, if you fertilize them at all.

As a general rule, dig and divide your bulbs every three years, ideally in the middle of their dormancy period. When bulbs are due to be divided, mark their location before they disappear so you will know where to find them. Some bulbs resent division, so adhere to local customs when deciding if and when to dig your bulbs.

Some gardeners never dig and divide and have beautiful displays. It all depends on how the bulbs grow in your particular climate and soil. Note that bulbs that do great in the damp climate of the Southeast, such as cannas and crinums, may have problems in drier areas, where alstroemerias are a better choice. An exhaustive list of promising bulbs for warm-climate gardeners would be too long to include here, but following is a small sample that includes some well-known species:

* **Spring** — daffodil, tulip, narcissus, crocus, muscari, scilla, amaryllis

* **Summer** — alliums, calla lily, canna, crinums (some bloom in spring and fall), *hymenocallis*, gladiolus (all kinds), iris, lilies (tigers and Asiatics are easiest)

* **Late summer** — rain lilies, spider lilies, garlic chives (doubles as an herb), some crocuses

When choosing which bulbs to grow, lean toward those that bear simple single flowers of a modest size. The frillier and bigger the blossoms are, the more difficult it will be to get the bulbs to bloom reliably year after year. If you buy your bulbs in the fall, chill them in the refrigerator for a month before setting them out in January. That way, they will have no doubts that they've sat through the winter and will be off to a strong start after their season of rest. The exceptional cases are spider lilies *(Lycoris radiata)*, which enjoy their most active period of growth in the winter and are best planted in early summer.

HARDY ANNUALS AND BIENNIALS

These flowers receive considerable attention in my discussion of the biennial season (beginning on page 57, but I must re-emphasize how valuable these plants are to both landscape and gardener. These flowers are planted in late summer and fall, grow through the winter, bloom in spring, and then die.

From a landscape point of view, hardy annuals and biennials fill a flowering gap between spring-flowering bulbs and summer annuals. In addition, you can grow them without fighting the hot summer sun. Since they stay in the ground longer than annuals, they are good to locate near perennials that resent having the soil near them disturbed.

Following are eight of my favorites, along with tips for growing and using them:

* **Bachelor's button** *(Centaurea cyanus)* is tough, hardy, and great for cutting. Seeds can be sown where you want them to grow, or you can dig and move volunteers. Additional seeds may be sown in the spring to prolong the flowering period.

* **Chinese forget-me-not** *(Cynoglossum amabile)* is a half-hardy annual that can take light frosts but not hard freezes. If you live in a mild winter area, try to grow this lovely little flower, which bears dark, straplike leaves and dainty spikes of long-lasting little blue flowers. The 'Blue Showers' variety is a rare true blue.

* **Foxglove** *(Digitalis species)*, a true biennial, is great to use for a vertical accent in partially shaded flower beds. Grow them in clumps rather than rows for a natural effect. These may be direct-seeded or started in containers and set out after summer flowers have been pulled up.

* **Hollyhock** *(Althaea rosea)* is most often used as a backdrop plant because it is tall at the top and big at the bottom. Plants may live for two years or more, albeit in declining health.

* **Money plant** *(Lunaria species)* is not pretty enough for front-row use, but it is great for the side yard. Seedpods are easy to dry and use in flower arrangements. Money plants are very hardy and easy to grow.

* **Pansy** *(Viola species)* is the best fall-to-spring flower for eye-catching edging near entryways or other high-visibility spots. Enrich the soil with compost or rotted manure before planting. Seeds are slow to start but dependable. If you prefer, buy pansies as bedding plants.

* **Poppy** *(Papaver species)* is mostly perennial, although it often burns out in hot summer areas. Plant seeds very early in the fall where you want them to flower in the spring. Poppies are best when direct-seeded.

✳ **Wallflower** (*Cheiranthus* species) is among the most fragrant flower you can grow. They don't do well in acidic soil but otherwise require little care when grown from fall to spring. The orange-flowered *C. allionii*, or Siberian species, is very easy to grow, but showier *C. cheiri* varieties are certainly worth trying, especially where soil is naturally alkaline.

Easy Annuals

At last we come to the most popular, yet transient, of flower forms, the annuals. These grow relatively quickly, flower, and then die. Many of them can be purchased as bedding plants, while others must be started from seeds.

With annuals, you must plan on seasonal turnover, for few remain healthy and attractive for more than a few months. Although there are exceptions (ageratum, impatiens, and melampodium, for example), it's usually best to replace summer annuals once or even twice a year. For example, pansies may fill a high-visibility flower bed from fall to spring, then be replaced by petunias in late spring and dwarf zinnias in midsummer when the petunias fail.

To help you plan seasonal turnovers and annual special effects, consider the planting schemes in the box on page 143.

DESIGNING WITH ANNUALS

When working with annuals, think about whether you want a formal or an informal look. To go formal, you will use more straight lines and often repeat patterns of color and form. In informal designs, plants usually are grouped in clumps, clusters, or drifts so that one type of flower flows into the next.

Since annuals are the mixers and matchers of the flower world, often you will be using them to enhance, blend, highlight, or hide more long-lived plants. Use them to enhance temporarily a permanent fixture such as a mailbox.

In recent years, many annuals have become available in single, separate colors. We take for granted the chance to fill beds with lemon yellow zinnias or solid red impatiens, although our grandparents, who had only mixtures to work with, would think us very lucky indeed.

To make the most of this fortunate situation, try color coordinating an annual bed with several different flowers of similar color. For example, you can get zinnias and plume celosia in matching shades of yellow. Since the two flowers have different forms, they contrast even when they match. Add a third element that coordinates and contrasts, such as red-orange gomphrena, and you'll have a fantastic combination. Other possibilities include bright yellow and orange cosmos accompanied by orange marigolds, or pink-tinted strawflowers flanked by pink zinnias. Gardeners have long been mixing and matching flower forms and textures in all-white beds, but we're the first generation able to experiment with other common colors.

MIXING AND MATCHING COLORS

There is no magic formula to choosing compatible color combinations for annual flower beds. If you follow these four simple guidelines, your beds will look great.

FINE BEDFELLOWS

SPRING

Pansies with alyssum

Nasturtiums as cover for spring bulbs

Snapdragons with dwarf yellow marigolds

Petunias with slow-growing perennials

SUMMER

Abelmoschus alone in dry, sunny sites

Celosia with dwarf marigolds or zinnias

Cleomes in the back of the bed as a hedge

Cosmos (C. sulphureus) with soft yellow zinnias

Gomphrena as a replacement for biennials

Tall marigolds with dwarf ageratums

Melampodiums alone, as cover for resting daisies

Scarlet flax alone on a dry, sunny slope

Impatiens tucked between azaleas and rhododendrons

Portulacas as an underplanting for roses

Zinnia hybrids, in single colors, for a midsize border

FALL

Sunflowers in rustic colors with marigolds

Calendulas with purple pansies

Ornamental kale with color-coordinated chrysanthemums

---

* When working with a mixture that includes several colors, make a large planting of the mixture and complement it with only one other flower, with the second flower in a single color. For example, a riotous bed of mixed zinnias might be bordered with yellow Mexican zinnias, creeping zinnias *(Sanvitalia procumbens)*, or white vincas. Mixed impatiens might be accompanied by little white begonias.

* Separate single colors that might not match perfectly with white flowers or plants with gray foliage. These neutrals help offset potential clashes, and white goes with everything. (See the next section on filler flowers.)

* Don't be afraid of hot colors like red and orange. Especially in summer, the best annuals sizzle with these hues.

* Watch the depth of your beds. When a flower bed gets more than 4 feet across, include stepping-stones or a pathway. To create visual depth in a small space, use something very tall in the rear and a dark color in the front. In between, plant something of intermediate size. For example, plant bushy sunflowers in the back, zinnias in the middle, and red dwarf celosia in the front.

COOL BLUES

Like gardeners everywhere, warm-climate gardeners should be on the lookout for blue flowers. Blue flowers do an amazing thing when slipped in beside loud colors with high clash potential, like orange marigolds. In cool climates, various campanulas and lobelias, as well as mealy-cup sage *(Salvia farinacea)*, are commonly used for blue accents, but these will grow only as biennials in mild-winter areas and can't survive hot summers or very cold winters. If you find a blue you can use, do so with enthusiasm. 'Moody Blues' and other pansies, Chinese forget-me-nots, and myosotis can provide blue through the spring. In the summer, ageratums and blue flax are safe bets.

FILLER FLOWERS

A good flower must know how to get along with others. No flower exists alone. Flowers are planted to create visions that startle and excite but don't confuse the eye. As suggested earlier, you can soften potential conflict between colors and textures by using a neutral color such as white, gray, or soft yellow. If your flower beds seem to lack a polished appearance or look segmented or spotty, it's probably because they need neutral fillers.

The following flowers are the best candidates for warm-climate gardeners in search of visual unity. Once you get to know them, you will never be at a loss for quick cover-ups. As an added benefit, light-colored filler flowers shine in the moonlight, making them doubly attractive after dark.

* **Ageratum.** Resentful of drought, these flowers are otherwise easy to grow and provide a wonderful counterpoint for orange and red blooms. They are available in blue or white, dwarf or tall. In late summer, take cuttings and set them in damp potting soil; they will readily grow new roots.

* **Gypsophila.** Both annual and perennial forms create clouds of soft white or pink. These are great "blenders" for perennials with coarse leaves.

* **Portulaca.** When you can find these in all white or all yellow, use them in sunny beds as companions for red or orange flowers. They are especially good for planting around roses.

* **Dusty miller** (*Senecio cineraria* and *Artemisia stellerana*). At least a dozen flowers are better known by the common name dusty miller, with dusty white or gray leaves. Often they are perennial in warm climates, although plants look best if they are dug, divided, and replanted each spring.

* **Stachys.** Commonly known as lamb's-ears, these fast-rooting perennials can be plugged into partially shaded beds wherever

---

BRACTS VERSUS PETALS

If you want flowers with show-off potential that don't need a lot of water, look for those that have tiny flowers among larger, colorful bracts. Papery bracts require only a fraction of the moisture that petals do. Most of these also dry well for use in everlasting arrangments. The trade-off is little or no fragrance. The following are good bets:

Acroclinium
Gomphrena
Gypsophila
Statice
Strawflower
  (*Helichrysum* species)
Talinum
Zinnia

you need soft gray color. Propagate the leggy stems anytime from fall to spring.

* **Vinca.** Beware! If you plant these flowers once, you may never need to buy any others. Notorious for reseeding in warm climates, the volunteers come in very handy for filling in bare spots and covering for failing perennials and bulbs.

CONTAINER CANDIDATES

Many popular bedding plants, including petunias, geraniums, coleus, and even impatiens, are best grown in containers in warm climates. They will grow in closely tended beds, but their performance is limited by hot sun and dry soil. If you grow them in containers, conveniently located so you can water and feed them frequently, you may be amazed at their longevity and beauty.

In recent years, containers planted with an assortment of flowering annuals have become popular, and with good reason. Nothing brings grace to a porch, deck, or patio like large pots or boxes spilling over with colorful blooms. In dark nooks that receive little sun, try planting caladiums and impatiens together. If the colors coordinate well, the effect is breathtaking. Half a day of sun is all you need to keep petunias in bloom, provided you feed them every two weeks and keep the leggy stems pinched back. Coleus, set off with pink begonias or dripping stems of variegated vincas, makes a dramatic statement when grown in pots.

In addition, many flowering plants, known by old-timers as "porch plants," thrive in large containers or hanging baskets. One of my favorites is achimenes, or widow's-tears — tiny bulbs that spring to life in warm weather, bear beautiful monkey-faced blossoms, and become dormant when winter sets in. Containers planted with achimenes, caladiums, tuberous begonias, or other bulbs can be allowed to dry out and be stored, undisturbed, in a cool garage or basement through the winter. In the spring, you can replant them just as they are coming back to life.

When planting containers, use a

SEEDLINGS ON STANDBY

During long Sunbelt summers, your flower beds will be constantly changing as some plants burn out and others are eaten by bugs. It's great to have a few annuals growing in flats, pots, or cell packs to pop in where vacancies appear. I like to hold back a few yellow flowers, especially dwarf marigolds and melampodiums, which will wait patiently when left in small containers and seem to go with everything. Keep standby seedlings in semishade, and water and feed them sparingly to slow growth.

medium that will hold water well and
containers with plenty of holes in the
bottom. You can also put some rocks or
gravel in the bottom, if you like, to
improve drainage. When using packaged potting soil, add some peat moss
and a bit of compost to improve the soil's

IN-GROUND CONTAINERS
When planted in flower beds, impatiens, geraniums, and begonias are difficult to keep well watered. You may be able to solve this problem by planting them in containers (such as plastic nursery liners) and sinking them into the ground. Mulch them well.

ability to hold moisture. Then plug in your plants and start watering.

Every three weeks or so, fertilize all containerized flowers with manure tea
or another liquid fertilizer. Drench them well, for containerized plants do not
have the option of stretching their roots in search of food.

If, despite dedicated watering and feeding, your container-grown plants
start looking old before their time, repot or propagate
them. Stem cuttings of coleus, impatiens, ageratums, and many other container candidates
will quickly grow new roots when planted
in damp, gritty soil.

Should travel plans take you away
from home in the summer, put a small
plastic wading pool in a very shady spot
and fill it with your porch plants. Add
2 inches of water. Neighbors who fear
the responsibility of taking care of your
flowers will not be intimidated by instruc-
tions to replenish the pool's water once a week.

*Stem cuttings of many
annuals take root quickly in
damp, gritty soil.*

CONCLUSION

My intention in this chapter was not to describe strict recipes for flower gardens
but to whet your appetite for the many adventures that lie ahead for anyone
opening the big door into the world of flowers. I know I have named a hundred
flowers here, but don't interpret this to mean that you must break your neck
trying to grow them all. Instead, proceed slowly with new flowers, planting a
bed here and a pot there, and think of them as spotlights of color and form in
your yard and your life. With a little practice, you'll soon discover more and
more flowers that will come and go with your interests, which are certain to vary
from season to season and year to year.

Chapter Six

GRASSES AND
GROUND COVERS

NOT SO LONG AGO, before most of the lawn grasses and ground covers we know today had been imported and shared, and when people spent much more of their time outside, yards were mostly bare dirt, packed hard by the weight of a million footfalls. Instead of being mowed or raked, yards were swept. The Southeast, which was a lush forest before nonnatives started moving in, had almost no naturally occurring grasses to fill in open spaces, for grasses don't grow in shady forests. In the West, wild grasses did exist, but they couldn't tolerate the triple threat of high heat, scant water, and being stepped and sat on all the time.

I open this historical door to illuminate the naive spirit with which most of us approach the subject of covering our heavy-use areas with vegetation. Granted, we now have some wonderful plants to work with, but there is a natural conflict between growing plants and human use. No plant — grass or ground cover — wants to grow where people walk or play all the time.

You can, however, create plant carpets where you walk and play only some of the time. Air-conditioning has made this possible, for it has radically reduced the amount of time we spend hanging around in our yards. We don't rest beneath shade trees during the midday hours or remain outdoors through early evening, waiting for our houses to cool off. Today it's much easier to grow grass in sunny areas and ground covers in spaces shrouded in deep shade.

Neither group of plants — grasses or ground covers — will grow in spartan, compacted soil. The site must be prepared and improved just as you would for other plants. Dig or till, add organic matter and appropriate mineral fertilizers, rake out weeds, and then start planting.

What will you plant, a grass or a ground cover? There's a wild and totally unfounded notion that ground covers are easy and grasses are hard. Hogwash! True, you don't have to mow ground covers, but the trade-off is that they are slow to establish themselves, even when site preparation is meticulous, and they often need supplemental water. Both grasses and ground covers have their place, and finding that place requires nothing more than a sober look at the sites your yard has to offer. For example:

* You have a large swath of sunny space where the kids love to wrestle and throw the Frisbee. Plant grass.

* You have a big magnolia tree that casts heavy shade year-round. Grow a ground cover where a little light gets through, but forget about the space right around the trunk. It's hopeless.

* A small, cookie-cutter front yard is all that separates your house from the sidewalk or street. Shrubs and flowers hug the front of the house. Plant grass to make the yard look bigger and to highlight your larger ornamentals.

* You've planted some trees, but they are small. You don't want them hurt by mowers, string trimmers, or rowdy kids. Plant ground covers beneath them.

If you can't decide what to do in a given site, you can always install adjacent plots of grass and ground cover and see which of them does best. Grass usually will win out in sun, with ground cover being victorious in shade. In between, you may find wonderful little niches for ornamental grasses, various perennials, or perhaps a small outcropping of flat stones accompanied by a comfortable chair or bench. Before you resort to stone, consider the following discussion of lawn grasses, ornamental grasses, and ground covers for warm climates.

Lawn Grasses

Whether you want to or not, you must grow a little grass. Perhaps you really like lawns and want to grow a great one that looks like green velvet. Or maybe you'd be satisfied to let nongrasses mingle in a modest turf or, better yet, shrink your turf chores and maintain a smaller lawn of reasonable quality. Any person's interest in lawn maintenance is a question of degree: Many excellent gardeners care very little about it, while other folks who don't know a cactus from a coreopsis like to spend every Saturday mowing, feeding, and manicuring their lawns. It can be very sweaty work.

Growing lawn grass may not be very exciting, but other grasses are downright fun to work with. Ornamental grasses flow and sway their way through flower beds, fill in marginal spaces, or make nice specimen plants. In the latest shift in American garden design and tradition, spaces planted with lawn grasses are getting smaller, while the use of ornamental grasses is growing wildly.

It's about time. If the truth be told, green-velvet lawns are very difficult to maintain, especially in warm climates. I think people should think of lawn space only in terms of recreation and community standards. In other words, grow enough lawn in your front yard to blend in with the neighborhood (and remain friends with your neighbors) and enough in the back for a bit of private play space.

As for ornamental grasses, think of them as super-low-maintenance perennial flowers, for that's the niche they fill. But unlike flowers, which look really good only when they bloom, ornamental grasses bear watching as they catch the wind and either soften or intensify its motion practically year-round. Grass leaves and seed heads also make valuable filler material for fresh and dried flower arrangements. When it comes to upkeep, most ornamental grasses require nothing more than a yearly shearing in late winter to keep them tidy.

Both lawn grasses and ornamental grasses should be part of your gardening life. Of course, how much time and effort you spend cultivating them is up to you. I suggest thinking long and hard about the ease-of-culture issue before making decisions about which lawn grasses are best for your yard. With ornamental grasses, conjure up mental pictures of their special effects before you buy your starter plants.

TENDING TURF

With a few notable exceptions, all of the lawn grasses grown in warm climates are so-called warm-season grasses that green up in warm weather and become dormant when nighttime temperatures regularly drop below 55°F. Warm-season grasses vary tremendously in terms of upkeep. Not surprisingly, those that require frequent fertilization and a lot of water also tend to have the most refined appearance, while those that can take care of themselves don't look as luxurious. The choice is yours.

The various grasses you might choose are discussed in the following sections, but consult your Extension Service before making a final decision. Most of the better grasses are available in different varieties (and varietal blends) that are especially suited to local soil conditions and microclimates.

HIGH-MAINTENANCE WARM-SEASON GRASSES

Hybrid Bermuda

Very tight and low growing, hybrid Bermuda can stand heavy traffic, and the short leaves have a very even texture. This grass spreads rapidly, as the creeping stems knit themselves together into a fine carpet. Hybrid Bermuda produces few viable seeds and must be started from sod (you can stretch your dollars by cutting sod into pieces and planting the pieces). The shortcomings of hybrid Bermuda include a low tolerance for shade and a voracious appetite for fertilizer (feed it in April, June, and August). During periods of frequent rain, hybrid Bermuda also needs frequent mowing.

St. Augustine

This beautiful, shade-tolerant grass holds a vibrant dark green color when fertilized regularly. It is not hardy where winter temperatures often drop below 20°F, it needs a lot of water, and it likes acidic soil. Thus, its use is limited to semitropical areas that get plenty of rain. St. Augustine also has some serious insect enemies in some areas. It is planted from sprigs, which grow rapidly when set out in the spring and watered regularly.

Zoysia

Zoysia has a deep, cushiony texture and the look of luxury. Contrary to what its commercial promoters claim, however, zoysia is not a low-maintenance grass. If allowed to weaken for any reason (such as drought, physical injury, or a pest attack), zoysia loses its even texture and becomes invaded by weeds. In cold-winter areas where zoysia's natural period of dormancy is longer than five months, the leading invaders are wild onions and dandelions, which are both cool-season plants that grow while zoysia is dormant. In warmer places, nut grasses have an easy time colonizing zoysia lawns. On the plus side, zoysia does not need to be mowed very much, and it is a top performer where looks are all that really matter.

LOW-MAINTENANCE WARM-SEASON GRASSES

OPEN-POLLINATED BERMUDA

This grass grows wild over hundreds of thousands of acres in the Sunbelt. A few improved varieties developed in New Mexico have been released, but the most common strain is simply known as 'Coastal'.

The biggest problem with old-time Bermuda is that it enthusiastically invades flower beds, vegetable gardens, and even cracks in driveways and sidewalks. You must constantly dig out the wiry roots from places where you don't want them. If you never fertilize and never water a Bermuda lawn, however, chances are good that it will survive anyway. You have to mow it after every soaking rain in the summer, but during droughts it grows very little.

For resiliency in any type of weather and green appearance year-round, Bermuda may be oversown with tall fescue or annual rye. Where summer heat does not kill it, the fescue will persist from year to year and dominate in shady areas where Bermuda will not grow. In very hot summer areas, use annual rye for winter overseeding, since it is cheap and fast growing. Open-pollinated Bermuda may be planted from seeds, sprigs, or sod from spring through midsummer.

BUFFALO GRASS

This grass is fast emerging as a leading lawn grass in the West, where it is a native. Although basically a tufting grass, buffalo grass will form a nice turf in arid places, even with little or no watering after the first year. It looks best when mowed only sporadically so that it maintains

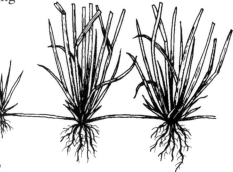

Buffalo grass

its soft, windblown allure. Buffalo grass often can be purchased as sod if you need grass cover quickly, or you can seed it in the spring. Use sprinklers to keep the seeded site moist while the seeds are germinating, then gradually reduce the water.

CENTIPEDE

Centipede continues to gain popularity in the lower South, where it grows well with no supplemental water (after the first year) and only slight fertilization. The acidic sandy soils of the Coastal Plain are no problem for centipede, which quickly covers the ground with ropy stolons. Although its color never gets darker than medium green, its beauty lies in its ability to survive high heat, humidity, and pressure from pests. Centipede's growth is so thick that it's difficult to overseed it with fescue or rye, so the lawn stays a mousy color through winter. Centipede can be planted from seeds (which are very tiny) or sprigs. Like other warm-season grasses, it is best started in the spring.

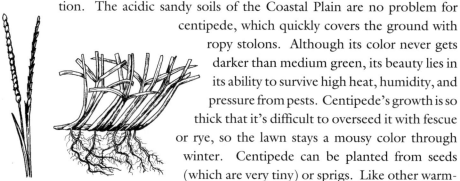

Centipede grass

BLUE GRAMA GRASS

This grass laughs at drought, as you might expect from a wild grass of the high western plains. If your yard is so dry that you can't imagine that any grass would grow there without illegal watering, try blue grama. During the first year after seeding, you have to trick it into forming sod by watering and mowing it several times; otherwise, it will grow up instead of out. After the first summer, put away your sprinkler.

Don't be fooled if blue grama dries up a bit in midsummer, for it will revive quickly after a rain. In hostile environments, allow blue grama to reseed, even if the seed heads make your yard look a little disheveled for a while.

COOL-SEASON GRASSES

Growing grasses that like cool weather in warm climates may sound silly, but it's not. In the upper South and many mountain areas, various fescues grow quite well from fall to spring and go dormant in midsummer. The most widely used one is **improved tall fescue,** which includes the open-pollinated 'Kentucky 31' and numerous improved varieties, including 'Rebel', 'Falcon', and 'Hawk'. All tall fescues are tufting grasses, but they make a very nice lawn and can tolerate quite a bit of shade.

Tall fescue lawns are normally started from seeds, although some of the newest dwarf strains grow so slowly that they are best purchased as sod. For improved winter color of thin Bermuda lawns, many people overseed with tall fescue in the fall.

Annual rye also can be used to overseed warm-season grasses, especially if you want quick results. One guy I know uses annual rye to write holiday greetings in his dormant centipede (do it in late October for readable boldness by mid-December). If your lawn suffers a terrible injury during the winter months, like when a truck loaded with firewood spins deep wheelies in the dormant grass, use annual rye to heal over the spot until you can repair it in the spring. Annual rye usually requires some mowing by midwinter, but summer's heat almost always kills it.

ORNAMENTAL GRASSES

If you look out your window on a cold winter's day, what do you see? If your eyes are fortunate enough to alight on some space manicured only by nature, perhaps you'll see tall fronds of dried grass nodding and swaying in the wind, despite the fact that they've already withstood the violent passage of several cold fronts. Wouldn't it be great to bring that drama of movement, plus a definable texture and symmetrical form, to vacant-looking places in your yard? That's exactly what you can do with ornamental grasses. Each ornamental grass has a slightly different look, but in general the choices boil down to three types of architecture, which I call flowing fountains, vertical waves, and jungle rugs.

FLOWING FOUNTAINS

Flowing fountains are big perennial bunch grasses that bear plumes that rise from the clump like sprays of water. The most popular one, pampas grass, makes an eye-catching specimen plant. Less riotous species, such as fountain grass, can be used as accents in mixed flower beds, as fillers in hot spots along sidewalks or driveways, or as backdrops for low-growing annual flowers.

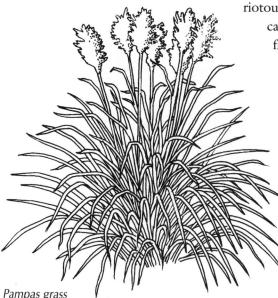

Pampas grass

These and other ornamental bunch grasses are very well equipped to cope with drought. When laid bare, the root systems look like jellyfish and almost always include several long, dangling threads that seek out moisture deep below the surface. As a unit, the bunched-up basal crowns do a nice job of insulating each other from scorching sunshine. Maintenance is limited to cutting back the clumps in late winter to make room for new top growth.

To start a clump, set out purchased plants in the spring and water them periodically the first year. When shopping for plants, be prepared to identify what you want by species names. Following are three well-known species to get you started.

Pampas grass *(Cortaderia selloana)*, originally from Argentina, is often a giant, growing to 12 feet or more, although a dwarf form called 'Pumila' grows to only 5 feet. Plumes may be white, pink, or beige, depending on the cultivar.

Fountain grass *(Pennisetum alopecuroides)* grows to 3 feet or more and bears rose-tinted hairy seed heads in late summer. This grass is extremely dramatic when planted in small accent clumps or massed in larger areas.

Silver grass is the common name of several species of *Miscanthus,* which can be quite large or grow to only 3 feet. These species need supplemental water in desert areas but generally are easy to grow. The seed heads are very feathery and quite attractive in flower arrangements.

VERTICAL WAVES

The grasses I think of as vertical waves are small and unremarkable when viewed as individuals, but if you put a bunch of plants together, you have an unforgettable sight. Before they develop tops, these grasses impart unique textural highlights as they catch dewdrops with their slender leaves. Later, the tops become flags that create vertical lines bending with each breeze and changing color with the seasons. Use these grasses as backdrops, as covers for slopes, or to frame evergreen shrubs. All you need is a space big enough to accommodate at least five plants and preferably twenty.

Several very well known ornamental grasses fit into this category. **Broom sedge,** the common meadow grass in the Southeast that goes unnoticed until winter, when it glows amber-orange in fields and pastures, makes a great accent when planted in a yard. Its botanical name, *Andropogon virginicus,* reflects its close association with **big bluestem** *(Andropogon gerardii),* a native cousin that's even taller (6 feet) and also widely distributed. **Little bluestem** *(Schizachyrium scoparium)* recently has been placed in a different botanical group, but it looks pretty much like a short (4 feet) version of big bluestem. Both go through a late-summer phase when they look somewhat blue, then fade to rusty brown in winter.

Quaking grass

If the *Andropogons* look too common for you, how about some **quaking grass** *(Briza maxima)* or maybe some **Indian ricegrass** *(Oryzopsis hymenoides)*? Both bear light, delicate seed heads that quiver in the wind, along with seeds much loved by birds. Quaking grass is winter hardy in most warm climates and often can be grown as a cool-season annual during the biennial season. Handled this way, it looks good just when everything else starts burning out in midsummer. Indian ricegrass grows well in dry, alkaline soil and usually is perennial in warm climates. Both of these grasses are reasonably small, topping out at less than 3 feet.

Finally, we come to ornamental fescue, which grows best during the winter months and thrives in partial shade. **Blue fescue** *(Festuca ovina glauca)* is easy to start from seeds sown in the fall, or you can start with purchased plants. It grows into hairy tufts less than a foot high and makes a great ground cover on windswept slopes. The color has a bluish cast, but most selections are best described as green.

JUNGLE RUGS

Jungle rugs are ornamental grasses that make good ground covers. They work best in partial shade and make me think of jungles, where each layer of plant life grows on top of the other, from the ground to the highest canopy. When the ground cover is a deep grass, a lush mood is created, along with good habitat for croaking frogs and chirping crickets.

Grasses in this category do have higher expectations in terms of soil and water than other ornamental grasses. For sure success, select a well-drained site in partial shade and enrich the soil with compost, rotted manure, or other rich organic matter before you set out the plants. Grasses in this group also can be grown in containers, where they provide fun foliage accents when set beside blooming plants.

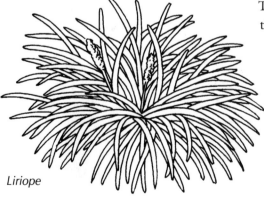
Liriope

The grass known as monkey grass, the most common grasslike ground cover for shade, may be one of two genera, *Liriope* (also known as **lilyturf**) or *Ophiopogon* (**mondo grass**). Except for the superior heat hardiness of mondo grass, there are more differences between varieties within the genera than between the two types of monkey grass. Generally, low-growing forms that spread willingly are the best choices for ground covers, with taller versions better used as edgings. The very small-leaved monkey grass often grown under old trees is usually *Liriope spicata*.

Both types of monkey grass are generally evergreen in warm climates, although either type may be injured by cold winter weather. When this happens, cut the yellow foliage back close to the crown (a string trimmer works best). Spring is the best time to scalp your monkeys. In summer, variegated versions may burn if not grown in substantial shade. Green monkey grass can take full sun, which encourages the development of small berries in late summer.

Both types of monkey grass are grown the same way. In spring, carefully divide clumps of purchased (or shared) plants into small clusters and replant them immediately, with the roots well covered. A mulch of chopped leaves scattered between the plants will hold the soil and discourage weeds until the grass takes hold. Look for noticeable spread the second year and a mature stand by the fourth.

Note that when lilyturf and mondo grass are used as edgings, they may need to be thinned back every few years. To do this, dig out excess plants by slicing downward through the middle of the clump with a sharp spade. Replant the divisions or give them away.

Various **sedges**, or *Carex* species, are increasingly used as ground covers in warm climates and are often substituted for monkey grass. These evergreen plants have the straplike leaves typical of grasses but grow into loose mounds that spread slowly via short stolons. Height ranges from 1 to 4 feet, depending on the species. Visit botanical gardens and fine nurseries to get a good look at these plants before you make plans for using them in your landscape. Leaf color varies from medium green to blue-gray to variegated (in Japanese sedge, which has yellow stripes).

If you have a place where the sun can illuminate a ridge of grass and the soil is suitably rich, try a wave of **Japanese blood grass** *(Imperata cylindrica rubrum)*. This grass grows in a low, spreading clump. The leaf tips are bright red, which explains the name. This is a warm-season grass that becomes dormant in winter. It needs several hours of direct sun.

Gardeners in other climates complain that **ribbon grass** *(Phalaris arundinacea)* is wildly invasive, but heat slows it down and keeps it in bounds where summers are hot. Also known as gardener's-garters, this grass's green and white stripes bring a cool look when it is allowed to ramble around old tree trunks. It is very easy to grow, provided you have both shade and water.

GROUND COVERS

Since broad-leafed ground covers need only to be trimmed from time to time and fed occasionally, and they never need mowing, they often are lauded as low-maintenance landscape plants. Once a ground cover becomes well established in a hospitable site, you don't have to put much effort into its upkeep beyond regular watering. But what does it take to establish a ground cover? Probably more than you think.

The task is difficult for several reasons. First, ground covers often are grown beneath trees, so from the beginning, the ground cover must compete with the tree for moisture, nutrients, and light. It's hard to improve soil that's thickly populated with tree roots. Frequently, the only really good planting holes will be scattered throughout the site rather than at regular 6-inch intervals (the standard spacing used for low growing ground covers). Indeed, a lack of planting pockets that can hold sufficient moisture to enable ground covers to establish a firm foothold can be an important limiting factor. Most ground covers do need quite a bit of moisture, which is why they are much more commonly grown in the East than in the West.

Finally, we come to the problem of human wear and tear, which young ground covers cannot tolerate. Only yesterday I saw a planting of pachysandra next to a school playground. It was barely alive and showed no signs of spreading, although it had been there for two years. The only hope for that pachysandra was a good fence or, better yet, the substitution of juniper or some other tough plants that don't mind sharing space with active children.

Unless you propagate your own plants in a nursery bed, you will need to buy quite a few ground cover plants to get started. Four plants per square foot is a reasonable estimate. If a friend or neighbor offers you all the vincas, ivy, or pachysandra you want, give the cuttings some time to develop roots before setting them out to fend for themselves. Sink the cuttings in a nursery bed or individual containers for at least a month and wait for new growth to appear before you plant.

DAFFODILS UNDER COVER

In many areas, daffodils suitable for naturalizing can be grown beneath ground covers, although you have to plant both (ground cover and bulbs) at the same time. If a tree is involved, it can't be an evergreen that blocks the sun year-round. The spaces beneath deciduous trees (which are bare in the winter) are ideal spots for daffodils interplanted with ivy, *Vinca minor* (vinca, periwinkle), or pachysandra.

HOT-NATURED GROUND COVERS

Vinca, also known as periwinkle and myrtle, is perhaps the best known and most versatile low, creeping ground cover. It comes in two forms. *Vinca major* is a large, sprawling, vinelike plant that runs on top of the ground and tends to be invasive. It can, however, be very valuable on rough slopes where nothing else will grow. The variegated form of *V. major*, often called white vinca, is very useful when combined with annual flowers in containers. In the course of one summer, runners 5 feet long may drip over the sides of the container and tickle the ground.

V. minor, or dwarf vinca, is a dark green evergreen. Because it grows so well beneath maples and other deciduous trees (even when the leaves that fall on it are never raked off), it's great for woodland areas, hard-to-reach rocky slopes, or island beds beneath trees.

Vincas also may be used to clothe the ground between irises and various perennials that are dormant for a long time, such as bleeding-hearts. Too much sun can cause vincas to burn, and you'll need to water them the first year. Once established, vincas will bear pretty blue flowers in late spring, though they are a subtle and short-lived show. As mentioned before, be sure the pieces you intend to plant already have a few roots, or the planting may fail.

English ivy *(Hedera helix)* is a woody evergreen vine that makes a fine ground cover and also will run up trees (and houses) with a little encouragement. It grows well in shaded courtyards and often is a miracle on erodible slopes beneath trees. Variegated forms are best in very deep shade. Although English ivy is slow to become established, mostly because its deep, woody roots take time to grow, it will persist for decades and can be hard to get rid of if you no longer want it around. In old cities, it's fun to look at the holly and ivy combinations that emerge around historic houses after both plants have been growing for more than fifty years.

Where **pachysandra** grows well, it imparts a lush look, shades out weeds, and rarely gets out of hand. Pachysandra is happiest in slightly acidic soil and is right at home in the partial shade around azaleas, small dogwoods, or even young magnolia trees. It will not grow at all on dry slopes, however, and always does best in a sheltered spot where the soil holds moisture well. For the best show, fertilize pachysandra in early spring. By midsummer, small, fragrant flowers should appear, followed by new leaf tips emerging from the ground in early fall. A variegated form is available. As with all white-leaved evergreens, it likes more shade than the green-leaved forms.

Regular ground covers may not have strong enough roots to hold a dry, unstable slope. Several other plants not normally thought of as ground covers may be just the thing you need. Following are three slope-management strategies that really work:

* Use daylilies. Their big roots and solid crowns hold loose soil well, and they're easy to plant. (Digging, weeding, and planting on a slope is treacherous unless you are gifted with great balance.) If you use mixed colors, be sure to include some early, mid-season, and late bloomers. Go with a single color if you want a more stately appearance. In mild winter areas, choose varieties that are evergreen.

* Junipers are very popular for slopes, and there's an easy way to plant them. Clean and cultivate the planting area, then cover it with a 1-inch layer of wheat straw. Plant the junipers, and then mulch between the plants (and over the wheat straw) with pine needles. The two straws will mesh together to form a tight mulch that looks good and covers bare soil until the junipers are large enough to do the job themselves.

* Roll out zoysia sod. If your slope is smooth and not too steep, plant lengthwise strips of zoysia sod in spring. Water it regularly for a couple of months, but don't mow it — just let it grow!

DRESSING UP SMALL SPACES

A number of other plants work well as ground covers in morning sun, including a few perennial flowers, such as creeping phlox, various perennial dianthus, and gold alyssum. Flowering vines also may be allowed to ramble at ground level, although care must be taken, or ground-hugging jasmine or wisteria will look like accidents. Passionflower vines rarely have this problem, and several common butterflies use them for a host plant. This vine's shortcoming is that is gives only summer cover and leaves the ground bare in the winter.

Three slow-growing ground covers are great for color accents in closely managed, high-visibility places. The first are plants in the *Epimedium* species, which need shade and rich, moist soil to make it in warm climates. Epimediums have lovely heart-shaped leaves tinged with red that are especially effective near entryways. Another crawler, *Lamium maculatum* 'White Nancy', can light up dark corners and contrasts beautifully with natural wood or stone. The 'Chameleon' strain of *Houttuynia cordata* looks like a tricolor ivy, although it is not evergreen. Pronounced "hot tuna," this ground cover lends an exotic summer touch to the spaces it fills; just don't forget to water it. All three of these ground covers also may be grown in containers and allowed to cascade over the sides.

CONCLUSION

Even considering all the neat grasses and ground covers warm-climate gardeners have to work with, there will still be bothersome pockets where naked dirt
insists on showing through and even nasty weeds refuse to grow. Perhaps the
place is too dark, too compacted, or too parched, or it's hiding a big rock just
below the surface. Whatever the problem, it's unlikely that either hard work
or good intentions will effect much change. Instead of trying to maintain a
cover of living plants in such a spot, reach for a bag of marble chips, polished
pebbles, or ground bark, or start collecting small stones and throwing them
there. A good ground cover does not have to be alive. If a puddle of pebbles
or basin of bark is surrounded by healthy, happy plants, that's good enough.
Place a small sculpture of a bunny or watchful cat in your trouble spot, and it
will surely come to life.

Chapter Seven

SOLVING PROBLEMS WITH PESTS

WHEN MY SON-IN-LAW WAS FIRST INVOLVED with composting but had not yet become a gardener, he toured my garden and asked a question I could not immediately answer: "What do you do when a bunch of insects shows up?" A native of southern Louisiana, Bobby grew up knowing the power of insects.

I thought of all the insect remedies I knew, and then admitted that mostly I do nothing. I named a couple of bugs — blister beetles and tomato hornworms — that I would pick off if I saw them. I showed Bobby hundreds of little holes in the leaves of my daisies and coreopsis made by a pest I had never dealt with before but had managed to identify as the four-lined plant bug.

"What does that mean?" he asked. My only answer was that somebody's food supply was ready. "Some predator will show up, and they will disappear," I said hopefully. Two weeks later, my prediction came true.

I don't know exactly what happened, but I do know that it will happen again and again and again. A month ago, little whiteflies came out of the lawn in clouds when I mowed. Now they are gone, along with the spring gnats that kept getting in my ears and the aphids that clung to the roses.

Who are the predators? I don't know, but I do know that I have to sweep down the porches often to keep the spider population within tolerable limits, and I must patrol the eaves of the house once a month to let wasps know that they can't nest there. You can find frogs in every flower bed, and garter snakes often rest in the cool dampness of the rainspouts. The world may be full of pests, but it's full of predators, too.

Unfortunately, pests and predators cannot be divided into neat little categories. Predators prey on each other as well as on pests. For example, paper wasps kill thousands of caterpillars to feed to their young, but they also kill spiders and just about any kind of larvae they happen to find. Blister beetle adults eat tomato leaves, but the larvae eat grasshopper eggs. As garden managers, we are constantly discovering small pieces of the complex web of life that exists in the natural world of our gardens. Many times it is wise to wait, watch, and live and let live. Other times it is prudent to declare all-out war against our garden's enemies.

Frequently, the pests that cause the most damage are those that have special talents for zeroing in on target plants. There is a certain symmetry here. Diseases and insects that focus on specific valued plants are the ones that cause us, in turn, to galvanize our intellects and come up with workable controls.

Warm-climate gardeners must spend more time on pest control than gardeners in other places because we have more pests to control. Mild winters result in minimal winter-killing of insect larvae and fungal spores. In dry areas, well-watered gardens may be the best places for insects to find something to eat or a place to lay their eggs. It's a sometimes unhappy paradox that the best places to grow plants also are the best places to find hungry insects and sneaky diseases.

CONTROLLING GARDEN PESTS

Keeping garden pests at bay involves the following five-point strategy:

* Cultivate a diversified mix of healthy plants grown in healthy soil.

* Use plants that can resist common enemies.

* Encourage natural predators.

* Use physical barriers to halt pest movement.

* Use gentle yet specific chemical controls.

DIVERSITY

From the tiniest bacteria to big, fat tomato hornworms, all garden pests require specific hosts. The more you change plants and soil treatments in space and time, the harder it is for many pests to gain a foothold. Many pests, like root-eating maggots, have very limited abilities to move from place to place, but you can easily move their preferred hosts. Since each space in a warm-climate garden is often replanted several times a year, there are plenty of opportunities to confound pests that get a start on one plant but cannot survive on another.

Rotating crops, using compost as medicine for suffering soil, and cultivating the organic content of the soil are discussed in Chapter 1, but all deserve reemphasis here, since the same things you do to create soil that's great for growing plants also makes the soil less hospitable to plant pests.

In your own backyard, you don't have to carry the concept of diversity to extremes by growing unrelated plants side by side in an attempt to thwart possible pests. Home gardens are pretty diversified by nature, especially if you contrast them with hundred-acre fields that are continuously planted in the same crops.

Of course, it can help a lot if you have several diversified sites in your yard — shady corners; windblown slopes; low, wet places; and sunny, open areas — for pests prefer different ecological settings. For example, spider mites love full sun, while slugs and snails prefer damp shade. If you rotate crops, care for your soil, and plant many different things, your garden should be wonderfully confusing for pests.

NATURAL RESISTANCE

Plants resist pests and diseases in many different ways. When insects eat tomato leaves, the plants respond by changing their leaf sugars, thus making themselves less appetizing. When a virus enters a pepper leaf, the plant will try to drop the leaf before the virus can invade the rest of the plant. Nature has many other ingenious tricks, many of which have been recognized and exploited by plant breeders. Choosing species and varieties that have special genetic equipment for tolerating or resisting pests is a gardener's most potent tool for growing a healthy garden.

What types of resistance do you need? Usually as much as you can get. All Extension Service offices offer lists of recommended varieties, which have been chosen with pest resistance in mind. Unfortunately, these lists go out of date fast, and many nonlisted varieties may be every bit as good (and more interesting) than those on Extension lists.

New is also better when your objective is to find the most pest-resistant varieties. For a long time, resistance was available for plant diseases but not for insect pests. This is changing fast as plant breeders screen and backcross various breeding lines based on their attractiveness to insects. New standards are set every time a new variety that can resist a new insect or disease is released. By seeking out the newest bean, sweet potato, tomato, or black-eyed pea, you are likely to get the best pest resistance.

When you're looking at disease-resistant varieties in seed catalogs, first consider varieties that offer a long list of protection. Contrary to common belief, resistant varieties per se do not taste bad. Thirty years ago, it was true that the best disease resistance was available only in commercial cultivars, bred to put up with rough handling and the rigors of shipping. But today plant breeders go to a lot of trouble to make sure new disease-resistant varieties taste as good as their nonresistant counterparts. As George Park, Jr., once told me, disease resistance has nothing to do with fruit quality. "All it means is that the plants will have a better chance of growing and producing for a long, long time," he said.

This does not mean that you will not occasionally get fantastic results with heirloom or nonrated varieties. Many old varieties are resistant to pests,

---

SHOPPING FOR RESISTANCE

The following diseases are common in warm climates. Resistant varieties of the vegetables named here are widely available.

Tobacco mosaic virus (TMV), which affects tomatoes and peppers

Fusarium wilt (F), a soil-borne fungus that affects tomatoes, cantaloupes, watermelons, beans, and other plants

Root-knot nematodes (N) on southern peas and tomatoes

Verticillium wilt (V), a fungal disease of tomatoes and eggplant

Maize dwarf mosaic virus (MDMV), which causes stunting and low production in corn

Smut (S), a disfiguring disease of corn

Downy mildew (DM), a common disease of cucumbers, cantaloupes, fall cauliflower, and fall spinach

Powdery mildew (PM), especially prevalent on cantaloupes and cucumbers

Curly top virus (CTV), a problem on western-grown beans and tomatoes

Cucumber mosaic virus (CMV), seen mostly on cucumbers

Resistance to several common garden insect pests is also available:

Cucumber beetle resistance is found in cucumber varieties described as nonbitter or lacking the bitter gene (it attracts the beetles).

Cowpea cucurlios are deterred by tough pod walls that keep them from penetrating resistant crowder and black-eyed peas.

Wireworms, flea beetles, and white grubs avoid resistant varieties of sweet potatoes.

Corn earworms cannot enter long husks that cover the tip of the ear. The husks create resistance via a physical barrier.

although that resistance has not been scientifically proven. Making use of all forms and degrees of disease resistance is the most painless and surest way to keep plant pests from taking a big bite out of your garden's bounty.

PLENTY OF PREDATORS

Beneficial insects are those that eat or parasitize other insects. Plenty of beneficial insects and larger predators mean fewer harmful insects live happily in your garden. The most beautiful way to encourage beneficial insects to live in your yard is to grow flowers, especially those that produce a lot of pollen. Honeybees, small wasps, predaceous flies, and other small beneficial insects love flowers, although their hunting grounds will certainly include nearby vegetables and fruits.

Besides food, beneficial insects need habitat. For this, try to incorporate perennial plants, such as a hedge of rosemary (for spiders), a clump of borage (for bees), and a small collection of shrubs (for mantises, assassin bugs, and other loners), into your landscape.

You can also invite large predators like toads and birds by providing homes for them. When a clay flowerpot breaks, use it as a frog house by placing it upside down beneath your tomatoes (frogs love the cool dampness there). Erect a house for purple martins or sparrows near the garden's edge, and let them eat your bugs for you.

Snakes also are a good sign. It has taken me a while to get over my natural fear of snakes, and I'm still wary of them. But, by learning which snakes to watch out for, I've been able to accept that the snakes that turn up in my garden won't hurt me. Usually they are garter snakes, although a giant king snake once sent me running for my reptile book. (It turned out to be a mighty predator.) For those of you who can't imagine *not* being afraid of snakes, you might want to avoid thick, continuous mulching. Snakes like thick mulches, as do the mice they like to eat.

Finally, consider incorporating a beneficial border or beneficial island into your garden's design. This might be a collection of perennial flowers and herbs

> ### STRIP STRATEGY FOR HOSTING BENEFICIALS
>
> At the USDA's research station in Tifton, Georgia, scientists have gotten good results planting cantaloupes and cucumbers in strips cut into established cover crops. In a large garden, you can try this yourself by planting a cover crop made up of a mixture of plants, such as winter rye, legumes, vetches, and turnip greens, and then cultivating large strips for planting. Beneficials that live in the cover crop patrol the cultivated crop and keep populations of insect pests seriously depressed.

or any plant grouping that offers year-round shelter for little carnivores like spiders and wasps. Notice which plants seem to attract these garden watchdogs, and group them together in a strategically located hedge or mound. That way, when you cultivate adjoining space, the predators will have somewhere to run and hide.

In addition, hundreds of much smaller beneficial insects live in warm climates, both above and below the ground, although they are very difficult to identify without a magnifying glass. Part of your goal in growing a healthy garden is to rear crops of these very useful insects.

The question of whether you should buy beneficial insects to release in your garden is a good one. Many well-known predators are now available as eggs or larvae, but putting them to work involves much more than simply opening a package and setting them free. Unless an abundant food supply is ready and waiting, chances are good that purchased beneficials will quickly fly away from your garden. Also, if weather conditions are not just right, the larvae may die soon after their release. As a general rule of thumb, purchased beneficials are most useful in enclosed greenhouses, where they can't slip away, or in large plantings of a single crop that has become seriously infested with a certain pest. For example, if you have more than a quarter acre of beans that are seriously infested with Mexican bean beetle larvae, it may be worthwhile to release Pedio wasps, an effective predator of this pest.

For most home gardeners, a better strategy is to grow small plots of plants that beneficials particularly like, such as alfalfa, tansy, dill, or buckwheat. Since bug behavior varies with climate and location, observe closely which beneficials turn up where. When my sweet corn tassels, ladybugs appear in large numbers.

THE BEST BENEFICIALS

In a healthy, diversified garden, you will see dozens of insects patrolling plants and mulches. Many of them spend their lives eating other insects or chewing up dead plant parts. Some insects in this huge group, known as beneficials, are quite famous for the good work they do keeping other insects in check. A small sample of these follows:

Big-eyed bugs, which resemble squash bugs, only with bulging eyes, eat other insects' eggs and small larvae.

Ground beetles, with shiny blue, black, or green backs, devour numerous soft-bodied creatures like slugs, cutworms, and root maggots.

Lacewings, known by their slender bodies and long, translucent wings, prey on aphids and other small, soft-bodied insects.

Ladybugs, also known as ladybirds and lady beetles, are the familiar red beetles with black heads that consume large numbers of aphids, mealybugs, and spider mites.

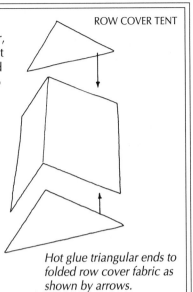
When my melampodiums bloom, they are covered with tiny wasps during the morning hours. By noting which of your plant favorites are popular with beneficial insects, you can easily increase beneficial populations by growing hospitable plants.

PHYSICAL BARRIERS

In situations where natural resistance does not exist and predators are no match for the pests, look to physical barriers that keep pests from reaching their desired host plants. The best example is floating row cover — lightweight sheets of spunbound polyester that can be placed over plants. Sunlight and rain pass through row cover, but insects can't. For numerous pests, including cucumber beetles, squash borers, carrot rust flies, aphids, and grasshoppers, floating row cover beats any other method of prevention or control.

Other physical barriers to use in the garden include cardboard cutworm collars (discussed on page 176), stem wrappings to keep squash borers from laying

To discourage slugs, rim plants with diatomaceous earth.

eggs in each plant's basal stems, and ribbons of wood ashes or diatomaceous earth to keep slugs from invading the strawberry patch. Some plants outgrow their susceptibility to pests, and keeping them under milk jug cloches may give them the head start they need. For example, if you keep eggplant cloched and then use row cover for a few weeks, flea beetles will not harm the plants until they are old enough to defend themselves.

Of course, the ultimate physical barriers are your own fingers. Pluck bugs from their hiding places and squash them, drown them, or coat them with oil. Some bugs are more pickable than others. Caterpillars can't escape when you go after them, and they usually leave a trail that makes them easy to find. But grasshoppers leap away when they sense your presence, and cucumber beetles easily fly to freedom. When attempting to handpick mobile insects, do it with a net and swoop down before the bugs know what hit them.

Many gardeners report success gathering bugs with hand vacs (portable, rechargeable vacuum cleaners). The trick is to empty the collection chamber frequently and to work methodically. Where many big bugs, such as squash bugs or blister beetles are present, try laying a cloth on the ground, shaking the plants so many of the bugs drop off, and then sucking them up.

GENTLE CHEMICAL CONTROLS

In every garden, a time will come when you can't stand the presence of a pest any longer and you must spray or dust it away. The following naturally derived pesticides are an organic gardener's big guns. With luck, you will rarely need them. Still, it's a good idea to keep these emergency supplies on hand (on a high, childproof shelf, always in their original containers).

Bacillus thuringiensis (Bt) is a naturally occurring group of bacteria that make pests sick after they eat them. The first and most common strain, *B.t. kurstaki,* will control just about any soft-bodied caterpillar found eating leaves — cabbageworms, tomato hornworms, fruit-tree leaf rollers, gypsy moth larvae, and so on. It is available as a dust, a liquid, or granules (for sprinkling on the tips of ears of corn for earworm control). A second Bt strain, *san diego,* is effective against the larvae of Colorado potato beetles. If you have a still-water pond on your property, you might use a third Bt strain, *israelensis,* to keep mosquitoes and blackflies from breeding there. All three forms are considered harmless to humans when used according to package directions. In addition to what it says on the package, avoid getting Bt in your eyes or in any break in your skin, and don't breathe in the dust. After all, these are living bacteria that your body considers sinister aliens.

Rotenone or **pyrethrin-rotenone** mixtures are the most potent naturally derived pesticides you can get, and they are extremely poisonous to fish, frogs, and people as well. They kill hundreds of species of insects and are toxic to an equal number of beneficials. I don't recommend that you depend on this class of chemical for protection of garden crops, but it's up to you. Just because they are derived from plants (and allowed by most organic certification guidelines) does not justify their routine use. Rotenone alone will kill just about anything if given a day or two to work. Pyrethrin paralyzes pests instantly and is known for its knock-down ability. I use it to keep paper wasps from nesting over my doors or on my porches, and I have used it for underground nests of yellow jackets. For the occasional wasp that slips into the house, I use hair spray to slow it down, then finish it off with a good swat.

Sabadilla is considerably safer than rotenone and provides excellent control of hard-backed insects such as squash bugs and blister beetles when they are too numerous to handpick. It has a shelf life of many years. Be very careful not to breathe in the dust, or you will sneeze your head off.

Horticultural oil is used in the winter to suffocate scale (tiny sucking insects that often look like scaly sections of bark) and various small insects that cling to the stems and bark of trees and bushes. For good coverage, use horticultural oil when temperatures are above 40°F. Using horticultural oil in late winter can have a big impact on how many whiteflies, mealybugs, aphids, and mites emerge in the spring from numerous trees and shrubs. A good pressure sprayer is required for proper application of horticultural oil.

Soap contains fatty acids that repel and sometimes kill aphids and other small insects. Products described as insecticidal soaps may also contain citrus oils or other aromatics to enhance their punch. Insecticidal soaps are good to have on hand in case aphids or mealybugs congregate on treasured plants (especially indoor houseplants). You can make your own soap spray by diluting a few drops of dishwashing detergent in water.

KNOW THINE ENEMIES:
A GUIDE TO INSECT PESTS

One of the first things to realize about the insect pests in your garden is that, for the most part, they are nocturnal. While you are asleep, cabbageworms may be working over your broccoli and cutworms may be cutting down your beans. What you can see in the daytime is only a small fraction of what goes on in the wild outdoors. If you imagine yourself to be a dark-colored beetle or cricket, you can imagine how stressed out you would feel if you spent all day hanging around a garden in El Paso. It would not take long to figure out that you could live a better life if you didn't move around too much until the sun went down.

Most of the bugs you see in your yard are harmless, and those that do damage will likely appear in large numbers, all at once. In this section, I list the most common unwelcome guests that turn up in warm-climate gardens and the best ways to get rid of them.

APHIDS

With bodies the size of the head of a pin and needle-sharp mouthparts for sucking plant juices, these common pests weaken plants and sometimes transmit viruses. They are a favorite food of small predators, however, which often keep them in check. For a vegetable gardener, the worst thing about aphids is how they congregate on leafy greens that have wintered over in early spring. Spray a jumble of aphids with insecticidal soap, and another jumble will appear farther down the stem. Instead of trying to beat them, consider joining them by letting them have the topmost section of the plants and harvesting the aphid-free side shoots for yourself. If aphids get on your lettuce or other greens in the fall, mist the plants with a fine spray of water the day before harvest and wash the leaves in cool salt water when you bring them in. For flowers and houseplants, keep a package of ready-to-use insecticidal soap on hand to spray as needed on aphid-ridden stems.

BLISTER BEETLES

Large and black, with a soft abdomen and yellow or gray stripes down the back, these pests of tomatoes, potatoes, and melampodiums turn their heads and give you a dirty look when you move in to get them. They appear in groups in early summer to midsummer, rapidly eating leaves in the lower sections and midsections of plants. Shake them to the ground and squash them with your foot or suck them up with a hand-held vacuum. Rotenone will kill them, but handpicking also works well. When handpicking, either work very quickly or wear a rubber glove, as some people get skin reactions from the gooey insides of this pest.

CABBAGEWORMS AND CABBAGE LOOPERS

These little caterpillars eat leaves of brassicas in early spring and again in the fall. They are most numerous on collards, cabbage, broccoli, and cauliflower. Cabbageworms lie flat against leaves as they feed, while cabbage loopers have looping inchworm-type physiques. Both are moth larvae and are very easy to control using a Bt-based insecticide. If the infestation is light and your eyes are good enough to spot the worms, which are exactly the same color as brassica leaves, you can pick them off. Sparrows and other birds consider them delicacies. I have watched as a fellow's cabbage patch was worked by sparrows in the spring, leaving not one cabbageworm behind.

COLORADO POTATO BEETLES

This very serious pest of potato plants is seen year after year in many home gardens. When they can't find potatoes, these beetles may settle for tomatoes, peppers, or eggplant. In the spring, the adults emerge from their winter hideouts below ground ready to find mates and start laying eggs. They are orangish tan with black stripes and a spotted head. Grab every one you find. The pale yellow eggs are very difficult to spot on the lower sides of potato leaves or hidden deep inside growing tips.

When potato plants are just getting ready to blossom, expect a population explosion. Handpick the soft-bodied, red-orange larvae daily. Or, you can treat affected plants with a special strain of Bt, *san diego*, provided the larvae are young. Be sure to get the stuff down inside blossom buds, where tiny larvae often are numerous.

CUCUMBER BEETLES

Whether striped or spotted, these small yellow and black winged beetles pose a triple threat to cucurbits and may infect other vegetables with cucumber mosaic virus. They emerge in the spring, and populations build all summer until the cold weather kills them or runs them into hibernation in weeds and tree crevices. The striped ones carry bacterial cucumber wilt, a disease for which no resistant varieties exist. Larvae of spotted cucumber beetles are known as western corn rootworms. Both spotted and striped cucumber beetles prefer to feed on the leaves and stems of cucumbers, squash, and cantaloupes (bitter compounds in cucurbit leaves, called cucurbitacins, actually stimulate beetle feeding). They lay their eggs in the soil below the plants, and larvae soon emerge and start chewing on the roots.

Row cover works well in keeping the beetles at bay, especially when plants are young and most susceptible. A few varieties of cucumber lack the bitter gene that makes leaves such palate pleasers to the beetles. You can also try trapping cucumber beetles using cucurbitacin-rich cucumber peelings or cantaloupe rinds as bait. Place the rinds in a shallow container and douse them with poison (rotenone or pyrethrin) or lace them with supersticky Tanglefoot. Replace the traps every few days.

CUTWORMS

The heartbreak of finding the tomato seedlings you've nurtured on the windowsill for a month felled like little trees is something every gardener experiences at one time or another. The culprits are cutworms — larvae of the large, pale moths that flutter around your porch light at night. Many moth species are involved in this seedling sabotage, which tends to be worst on seedling beans and various tender transplants reared indoors. You will never actually see a cutworm in action unless you go out at night to find them. Like so many other pests, they do all their dirty work after the sun goes down. By daybreak, they have hidden themselves in the soil and curled up to rest.

In a small garden, you can prevent cutworm damage by equipping transplants with stiff paper collars. I make mine by cutting the bottom out of small paper cups and pushing them into the soil around each plant. Milk jug cloches, pushed at least an inch into the soil, offer similar protection. Cutworms are often very bad in soil that's previously been covered with grass and is being used for vegetables for the first time. In this situation, you may want to try packaged parasitic nematodes, a rather recent innovation in cutworm control. Timing is critical with the nematodes, as they must have warm weather to thrive. When they do, they invade the cutworms' bodies and kill them.

FIRE ANTS

Fire ants rule many sections of the South, and if you live in their range, you may be in for trouble. They love the soft, cushy soil gardeners work so hard to create, and they have a knack for nesting in inconvenient places. Raised beds are frequent favorites, unless they are kept quite damp at all times. Fire ants seldom damage crops, although they have been observed eating okra. Still, they can make working in the garden unpleasant for adults and downright risky for children.

If your yard has only a hill or two of fire ants, pour a large pot of boiling water down the entry holes and follow up with repeat treatments as the colony tries to relocate near the old nest. Your local garden center or feed store may carry special fire ant poisons that are actually sterilants for the queen. You set out the granules, workers take them to the nest, and the queen eats them and becomes sterile. These products are often called growth regulators, and it may take two months to see the final results. Fighting fire ants is a constant task if you live in a heavily infested area. Scientists are working feverishly to find a reliable natural predator, such as a parasitic mite or nematode, but meantime your best strategies are to fight them with boiling water and hormones.

GRASSHOPPERS

Grasshoppers come in many different colors and sizes, and all are enthusiastic consumers of flowers, vegetables, and fruits. Some years are worse than others, and in bad years they are everywhere, eating everything.

To launch an organized defense against grasshoppers, begin by covering treasured vegetables with floating row cover. Next, plant a trap crop of marigolds (which grasshoppers love), get a small bug net, and start collecting grasshoppers off the marigolds. Set up a bird feeder in the middle of your garden area and offer an assortment of foods to attract different types of birds. Many eat grasshoppers. Finally, cultivate frequently to discourage egg laying in your garden.

If your area is plagued by grasshoppers every year, you might consider enlisting the help of your neighbors in controlling them with a parasitic protozoan called *Nosema locustae* (sold commercially as Grasshopper Attack, Semaspore, Nolobait, and others). This organism makes grasshoppers sick and kills up to half of them if you get it out in early spring, when the eggs are hatching. The next year, more will die from infected eggs. The stuff is inexpensive, but unless you can cover a wide area, it won't do much good. Grasshoppers can and will hop to your property from any untreated spot.

MEXICAN BEAN BEETLES

When one of these yellowish brown beetles with sixteen black spots lays her eggs on the underside of a pole bean leaf, she probably feels confident that her babies will live long, happy lives. Pole and bush snap beans are this pest's favorites, although they'll go for a lima or a black-eyed pea patch in a pinch. Mexican bean beetle adults nibble on leaves, but their main reason for hanging around beans is to find a mate. Once mated, they lay their eggs in small clusters beneath leaves. These eggs hatch into larvae in a week or two. The larvae then proceed to rasp the flesh from the leaves and devour it. They quickly grow into soft, spiny yellow-orange blobs. They leave behind leaf skeletons, which seriously weaken the plants. They also feed on bean pods.

The first line of defense is to plant your main crops both very early and very late. Early crops have plenty of time to grow before the adults start reproducing, and populations fall off (probably due to natural predators) in time for you to enjoy a pest-free fall crop of fast-maturing bush beans. Take out the early planting as soon as production falls off, and you may trap an entire generation before it can reproduce. In less fortunate circumstances, when the larvae are all over your beans and too numerous to handpick, try sabadilla dust to bring them under control. Rotenone, carefully dusted or sprayed on leaf undersides, is a sure cure.

SLUGS AND SNAILS

Both slugs and snails are slimy little creatures that chew holes in hundreds of plants, from spinach to strawberries. A few of them don't do much damage, but where there is one slug, there often are many more. A snail is little more than a small slug with a shell. If your garden is the dampest, lushest place around, that is where these pests will want to spend their evenings eating and their days resting.

Within the garden, you can limit slug hiding places by picking up boards left in walkways and keeping compost materials away from the main garden site. The next line of defense is to trap them. The most popular method is to set traps filled with something slugs like to drink, such as beer (even the nonalcoholic kind) or a mixture of 2 cups water, 1 tablespoon sugar, and   package dry yeast. Fill tin cans or plastic containers (such as deep margarine tubs) with the bait, then set them in shallow holes. The slugs will get so excited about the treat inside that they will fall in and drown. Empty and refill these traps daily.

To supplement traps, you can try various barriers that slugs don't like to cross. Among these are lime, diatomaceous earth, sawdust, and wood ashes. Such barriers lose their effectiveness after a rainstorm. Salt dehydrates slugs, but it's not the best thing to scatter around a garden. If you have a terrible slug problem and local zoning ordinances allow, the best slug-control device is a pair of hungry ducks.

Nobody likes handpicking slugs, but often it's the only way to get rid of them. When you're finished, remove the last traces of slug slime from your hands with baking soda or scouring powder.

SPIDER MITES

These tiny pests love hot, dry summers. They are too small for you to see well, but you can easily recognize the pale, microspeckled leaves that result when mites colonize leaf undersides. In midsummer, they may show up on vegetables, shrubs, and flowers, sapping the leaves of color and strength.

To banish spider mites, try modifying the environment by installing a sprinkler-type soaker hose beneath infested plants (use the flat kind with holes in it that spews up little fountains of water). This will make it easy to saturate leaf undersides once or twice a day, making the environment much less attractive to this pest. I have had some success using a commercial organic miticide made from citrus aromatics and water, and then covering the plants with a blanket for several days. This light deprivation seems to be worse for mites than it is for plants, and it gives the plants a brief period of recuperation after a bad mite infestation.

SQUASH BORERS

After this pest strikes, you will notice that some squash plants wilt more in the middle of the day than others. Closely examine the basal stem of wilt-prone plants, a few inches above the soil line, and you may see a tiny hole surrounded by loose, sawdustlike frass. This is actually the excrement of the most secretive enemy of squash, the squash borer. A fast-moving moth lays her eggs on or beneath the stem, and the eggs hatch into borers that eat the squash stem from the inside out. They hit in early summer and stick around until fall. Squash are normally so robust in their early growth that the damage is seldom seen until it's almost too late. If you use row cover to protect squash from other pests, you will be taking it off at just the time that borers are scheduled to start living it up.

Still, a squash-loving gardener can do several things to outwit this pest. First, hide the basal stem, either by wrapping it with bits of row cover or an old nylon stocking or by keeping dirt mounded up over it. With long-vined squash, encourage the plants to develop supplemental roots by sprinkling extra soil over their "elbows" — places where the stems naturally arch down to the soil. If borer damage is under way and you spot it early, try injecting liquid Bt into the stem where the borers are feeding (shoot it into the hollow center several inches above where you suspect the worms are hiding). You can also try slitting the stems lengthwise and removing the borers with tweezers. Then tie up the stem with string and mulch over the cut to keep the stem from drying out. Squash stems never really recover from such surgery, but they can handle clean slits better than prolonged borer feeding, which leaves them increasingly fragile until the plant finally dies.

SQUASH BUGS

Squash bugs vary in color from light brown to black, but all have the classic shield bug shape and are most threatening on summer and fall crops of cucumbers, squash, and cantaloupes. Populations build over the summer and are usually most prolific in early fall. If you have only a few plants and only a few bugs, handpick them by spraying the plants with water and immediately moving in with nimble fingers and a jar of hot water, rubbing alcohol, or vegetable oil in which to drop the bugs. You will find them hiding in the mulch under the plants' lowest leaves or clustered around the basal stem. Look for egg clusters on leaves and rub them off with your fingers. In severe situations, use sabadilla dust to get rid of squash bugs.

TOMATO HORNWORMS

These eating machines turn into beautiful sphinx moths, but not until they have devoured massive quantities of tomato leaves. Large and green, with diagonal white stripes on their sides and a soft horn on their rear end, tomato hornworms usually appear in early summer, after tomatoes have set fruits. In most warm climates, a second generation of hornworms will appear in time to damage fall tomatoes. Look for them wherever you notice missing leaves and a telltale trail of excrement. Handpick them or use a Bt insecticide if there are too many. Small wasps parasitize tomato hornworms, leaving noticeable white cocoons attached to the hornworms' backs. If you have some tomato leaves to spare, allow parasitized hornworms to live until the wasp larvae kill them and then set out into the world to kill other pests.

COMMON GARDEN DISEASES

Warm climates host a broad range of plant diseases. Many of them are difficult to identify positively, but the following information should help you make a reasonable guess as to what's gone wrong. In general, plant diseases fall into one of the following categories: soil-borne pathogens (nematodes, fungi, and bacteria that live below ground), leaf spot diseases (that attack leaves and stems), molds and mildews (which are like giant versions of leaf spots), and viruses. To help you make a proper diagnosis, let's look at each of these types of plant diseases.

SOIL-BORNE PATHOGENS

Fungi, bacteria, nematodes, and other soil-borne pests easily survive mild winters; avoiding them is a distinctive feature of gardening in warm climates. Some of these, including the strain of fusarium wilt that attacks watermelons and southern root-knot nematodes, defy absolute eradication. However, the following cultural methods, used in combination with resistant varieties, can suppress many soil-borne pests to tolerable levels.

* Rotate crops.

* Use compost as medicine.

* Raise the organic content of soil.

* Water wisely.

* Solarize soil prior to fall planting (see box on next page).

Now let's discuss the most common soil-borne pathogens in warm climates and the best ways to keep them under control.

NEMATODE NIGHTMARES

Nematodes are microscopic wormlike organisms that become plant parasites. Think of them as the pinworms of the plant world. The most common species, the southern root-knot nematode, parasitizes plant roots, often causing small galls, or knots, to form on plant roots. Okra is highly susceptible, as are tomatoes and carrots. Peppers and figs are moderately susceptible but will continue to grow if they are given plenty of water. Wounds made by nematodes often become entry points for other soil diseases, especially the fungi that cause fusarium and verticillium wilts. Nematode-resistant varieties of tomatoes and southern peas are available.

Unfortunately, the southern root-knot nematode has many cousins that are nastier and more aggressive than it ever dreamed of being. Some even parasitize the stems of woody shrubs. Nematodes are the undisputed rulers of the soil in many warm climates, and dealing with them requires constant vigilance and frequent compromise.

Several organic methods can keep nematodes suppressed so that you can grow all but the most susceptible plants. The most important thing is to cultivate quality soil that holds moisture well. When plant roots are as healthy as they can be and the plants are able to absorb water, they can often tolerate the presence of nematodes.

Nematodes are more active in warm weather than in cool weather. This means that the best time to deal them a lethal blow is late summer, when nematode numbers are highest and it's too hot to garden. Almost all the effective nematocides have been removed from the retail market, but they gave only temporary relief from nematode problems anyway. Nontoxic temporary relief is available in a process called soil solarization (see box below).

Beyond solarization, there are other ways to fight back nematodes. One very smart strategy is to add plenty of chitinous material to the soil, including shrimp hulls, crab shells, eggshells, and packaged products such as seafood meal and Clandosan. These substances attract microorganisms that eat chitin, which happens to be the same thing nematode eggs are made of. By supporting a teeming community of chitin-eating microcritters in your soil, you can limit the number of nematodes in future generations.

Also avoid any injury to plant roots. Don't squash roots by standing on them, cut into them with hoes or shovels, or otherwise cause breaks through which nematodes (and other soil-borne pathogens) can enter.

Not all nematodes are bad. You can purchase beneficial nematodes that parasitize and kill grasshopper and moth larvae. Mix them with water to bring them to life, and then sprinkle the mixture into infested soil. The timing is crucial, and soil moisture and temperature must be just right. Follow the

---

SOLARIZING SICK SOIL

When properly done, solarization will kill many of the nematodes, disease organisms, and weed seeds in the top 4 inches of soil. Do it in midsummer, when temperatures are very high, and just before fall vegetables and flowers are planted.

1. Cultivate a 10-foot by 10-foot plot.
2. Add a 1- to 2-inch layer of fresh manure and work it in well.
3. Shape the soil into ready-to-plant beds or rows.
4. Dampen the soil well.
5. Spread a sheet of heavy, clear plastic over the plot and bury the edges. The plastic should be somewhat loose, as it will balloon up with excess heat and steam.
6. Wait four to five weeks.
7. Uncover the soil, water it, and plant your crops. Do not recultivate before planting, or you'll bring untreated soil to the surface.

package directions precisely, and make sure the right pests are present before investing your time and money in these organisms.

As a final strategy against destructive nematodes, grow the most susceptible plants in containers and strictly limit the possibility that the soil in those containers will become contaminated with nematodes by keeping them up off the ground and filling them only with freshly sterilized soil. A splash of rain from nematode-infested soil is all it takes to start a teeming colony in a flowerpot.

> ### FLOWERING NEMATODE REPELLENTS
> In flower beds (or the vegetable garden, for that matter), keep nematodes unhappy by growing plants that nematodes can't stand. The best-known "starvation" crops for root-knot nematodes are African and French marigolds, but nematodes don't like salvias either. For the best results, plant these flowers in a solid mass so the nematodes will starve rather than going elsewhere in search of host plants.

TEXAS ROOT ROT

This fungus infects trees and shrubs where winters are warm and the soil tends to be alkaline and low in organic matter. Aboveground, you may see puddles of spores (which look like cake batter) oozing from the ground following summer rains. Underground, the fungus strips the outside of roots, rendering them useless for gathering water. The most common symptom is rapid wilting of leaves and branches on hot days. Growing resistant species, lowering pH into the normal range, and adding organic matter to the soil are the best preventive measures. Bamboo, bananas, cacti, citrus fruits, pomegranates, and rosemary are resistant. The most susceptible list includes stone fruits (peaches, plums, and apricots), figs, roses, and willows. See individual fruits in Chapter 4 for more information on resistant varieties.

PIERCE'S DISEASE

This soil-borne bacterium is a serious problem with grapes in many Gulf Coast states. It causes leaves to turn brown, followed by shriveled fruits and, eventually, dead plants. Growing resistant varieties is the only defense.

SOUTHERN BLIGHT

This fungus is often seen on peppers, tomatoes, and okra. Infected plants mysteriously wilt to death in midsummer, and if you look closely, you will see a mass of white mold at the base of the plant, right at the soil line. Typically two or three plants will die, but nearby plants will be unaffected. Adding organic matter to the soil, providing ample nitrogen, and soil solarization can help prevent this disease. Also keep mulches pulled back from the base of the plants so air can circulate freely around the basal stems.

FUSARIUM WILT

Fusarium wilt comes in many different strains, all designed to infect particular plants. This fungus strips the small feeder roots from plants, putting them under considerable stress. It is very common on tomatoes and watermelons in warm climates. Leaves turn a distinctive yellow as they wilt gradually over a period of weeks. Resistant varieties are widely available, although resistance may prove insufficient where nematodes facilitate the entry of the fusarium fungus. Poor drainage also encourages this disease.

VERTICILLIUM WILT

This fungus lives in many soils where cool conditions prevail during much of the year. Eggplant is highly susceptible and is often used as a test crop to see if this fungus is present. The fungus enters through plant roots and plugs up the plant's vascular system, causing it to wilt due to a lack of water. Resistant tomatoes are widely available.

LEAF-SPOT DISEASES

These diseases are most severe in humid areas where abundant moisture and heavy dews keep leaves damp for long periods of time, thus helping fungi to reproduce quickly. Picking off the first affected leaves can help, but there is no substitute for good morning sun. Never water susceptible plants in the evening, as nighttime moisture encourages these diseases.

EARLY BLIGHT

Early blight of potatoes and tomatoes is caused by alternaria fungi, which thrive on the hairy undersides of damp leaves, making brown dots that enlarge and run together until the entire leaf dies and drops off. Late planting can help, along with timely treatments with compost tea. Reliable resistance is not yet available but should be coming soon. Meanwhile, avoid determinate tomato varieties with curled leaves, as these seem to be the most susceptible. Also, don't plant tomatoes right next to or after potatoes, as early blight can spread quickly from one crop to another.

TREATING DISEASES WITH FERMENTED COMPOST TEA

Using compost tea as a disease inhibitor is a new idea that researchers in Germany, Alabama, and other places are just beginning to investigate. It appears that when you make an elixir from compost and water and apply it to plant leaves, the microorganisms within the "tea" compete with or devour disease-causing fungi and bacteria. Used in combination with resistant varieties, it may help prevent or treat common foliar diseases such as leaf spots and mildews. In my own backyard experiment, it helped blight-stricken tomatoes recover and gain enough strength to produce a good fall crop. Here's how to make it.

In a large bucket, mix 1 part manure-based compost with 3 parts water. Stir well and set aside to brew for three days. Stir again, strain through a piece of metal or polyester window screening, and then strain through cloth. Do this outdoors, for the mixture has a strong odor. Pour the mixture into a spray bottle and thoroughly wet both sides of the leaves with a strong stream of tea. Use leftover tea as fertilizer for containerized plants. Dump the solid residue in the garden. Repeat every two to three weeks.

CERCOSPORA

This leaf spot affects beets, southern peas, peanuts, and some beans in humid climates, causing dark, circular spots with raised centers. It is sometimes called frogeye. Sometimes whole leaves become spotted and drop off. This disease weakens, but seldom kills, plants. Resistant varieties have recently been released and should become increasingly available.

RUST AND ANTHRACNOSE

These two leaf spots are difficult to tell apart, and both are common on beans. In addition, anthracnose infects cucumbers and watermelons in humid areas, causing dark, elongated spots on the undersides of leaves. Both diseases are spread by wind and rain. Resistant varieties are widely available.

MOLDS AND MILDEWS

These diseases are also caused by fungi, but the organisms are unusually large and easy to identify. Thorough cleanup of plant debris is required to interrupt the life cycles of these organisms. Also gather up and compost mulches that may host the organisms.

BROWN ROT

This disease affects peaches, plums, cherries, and grapes in many warm climates, resulting in fruits that are covered with a brown fuzz just as they approach ripeness. Gather up all infected fruits and burn or bury them. Prune the trees or vines to encourage good air circulation and penetration of sunshine.

Some modern plums developed by Auburn University and prefixed with AU are slightly resistant. Muscadines are more resistant than bunch grapes.

DOWNY MILDEW

This mildew comes in hundreds of strains that attack various crops from broccoli to spinach. The tops of leaves show yellow patches, and below these patches you can usually see sections of gray or bluish fuzz. The disease tends to be worst in the fall, during cool, damp weather. Resistant varieties are widely available.

POWDERY MILDEW

Powdery mildew does not require abundant moisture, as the fungi that cause the disease sink rootlike sucking organs, called haustoria, into plant leaves. A powdery growth appears on the surface, making the leaves look as though they are dusted with flour. Fruits of affected cucumber and cantaloupe plants taste terrible. Choose resistant varieties.

VIRUSES

More than six hundred viruses that cause plant diseases have been identified, resulting in a confusing assortment of symptoms. Some viruses, such as tobacco mosaic virus, can be spread by the wind or a human touch, but most require the presence of an insect vector. Most of the typical vectors are very small. They feed by sucking plant juices and can live quite happily under very dry conditions.

The situation is aggravated in warm climates, where vectors such as whiteflies, aphids, and thrips may have as many as ten generations a year. Because of the increasing populations of vectors, viral diseases become more widespread as the summer wears on and are most severe in early fall. Since these insects are so tiny and mobile, insecticides are often ineffective in controlling them. Row cover can offer good physical protection, but the best defense against these diseases is to plant resistant varieties. It also helps to pull up infected plants as soon as they are identified so that there will be fewer viral spores for vectors to pass on to other plants.

The following four viruses are common in warm climates. Many others show similar symptoms in plants.

MOSAIC VIRUSES

These include tobacco mosaic virus and cucumber mosaic virus. They cause a distinctive curling of the leaves along angular lines. Fruits are often streaked and misshapen. The fruits are edible, but don't save the seeds, as viruses are often carried on them. Resistance is available in tomatoes, peppers, and cucumbers, but not in squash. Squash infected with cucumber mosaic virus will bear, but yields will be reduced and yellow summer squash may have green streaks.

CURLY TOP VIRUS

This virus is usually limited to western areas where beets are also grown. Tomato plants become stunted and may bear clusters of infertile flowers surrounded by crinkled leaves.

POTATO VIRUS Y AND TOBACCO ETCH VIRUS

These two viruses often infect peppers in warm climates, although the only symptoms may be reduced vigor and yield. Resistant varieties are increasingly available.

CONCLUSION

I hope that this lengthy discussion of garden pests has not tricked you into believing that pests, by their nature, have the upper hand in warm-climate gardens. They don't, because you are smarter than they are. Besides having your own brain to work with, you have the know-how of countless generations of horticultural thinkers on your side in the war against pests.

Sometimes you may lose a battle, but not without learning an important lesson from it. Next time, that pest will encounter a more formidable enemy, for every tidbit of knowledge you accumulate will work to your advantage. As your soil improves over time and your collection of pet plants continually becomes more eclectic, your yard itself will become more pest resistant. There is very little about gardening that is instant. A strong, resilient garden grows with its keeper.

Chapter Eight

REGIONAL RESOURCES

GOOD GARDENERS NEVER STOP WONDERING, asking questions, and learning new things. Part of gardening's payback is that it keeps your mind alive. An active mind is like a compost heap: Give it many different ideas to work with, mix well, and old ideas are magically transformed into exciting new thought combinations.

The following list of regional resources has been compiled with this in mind. Not one of these seed companies, nurseries, books, and organizations is boring; every one has a unique viewpoint and plenty of ideas to make your gardening more fun.

First I must emphasize that your best friend in gardening is someone local — an Extension Service agent, Master Gardener, knowledgeable friend or neighbor, or nursery person. Don't be shy when you have a question. Asking someone who knows is always the best and fastest way to get an answer.

The seed companies and nurseries listed here all handle mail orders, but local garden centers also can be wonderful sources of seeds and plants. Ask your Extension Service agent and fellow gardeners about nurseries within driving distance and go see them. All good plants don't come in a box. By examining the merchandise yourself, you'll get a much better feel for any plant's overall health and appearance. Unless otherwise stated, catalogs are free from these reputable dealers.

Seeds and Plants

VEGETABLES AND FLOWERS

Bountiful Gardens
19550 Walker Road
Willits, CA 95490

A nice collection of heirlooms and nonhybrids, each carefully evaluated before being offered for sale. Catalog, $1.50.

Burpee Gardens
300 Park Avenue
Warminster, PA 18974

One of the oldest names in American gardening remains a fine source of high-quality varieties.

The Cook's Garden
P.O. Box 535
Londonderry, VT 05148

Lots of European vegetable varieties here, and plenty of lettuce. The lettuces include hard-to-find winter-hardy varieties that will stand for months in warm-climate winters. Catalog, $1.

Hastings
P.O. Box 115535
Atlanta, GA 30310-8535

New and improved, this company's selections now include heirloom flowers and shrubs, along with disease-resistant vegetables and easy-to-grow flowers. Selected for the Southeast.

J.L. Hudson, Seedsman
P.O. Box 1058
Redwood City, CA 94064

If you're looking for something unusual that can be grown from seed, and you know the plant's botanical name, chances are good that J.L. Hudson has it. The company slogan, "Preservation through Dissemination," hints at the international collection of species offered. The 95-page catalog, $1, is a valuable reference for plant seekers and collectors.

Johnny's Selected Seeds
Foss Hill Road
Albion, ME 04910

Johnny's specializes in varieties for cold climates, but its fast-maturing, disease-resistant varieties also are valuable where spring and fall pass very quickly.

Kilgore Seeds
1400 W. First Street
Sanford, FL 32771

Seeds selected for their ability to grow in Florida. Catalog, $1.

Liberty Seed Co.
P.O. Box 806
New Philadelphia, OH 44663

A general vegetable seed company, but Liberty does a remarkable job of selecting top-yielding, disease-resistant varieties while keeping a collection of worthwhile heirlooms.

Native Seeds/SEARCH
2509 N. Campbell #325
Tucson, AZ 85719

Native seeds of the Southwest and Mexico, meticulously collected and propagated with long-term preservation in mind. Catalog, $1.

Nichols Garden Nursery
1190 North Pacific Highway
Albany, OR 97321

Despite its northwestern orientation, Nichols sells many fast-maturing vegetables, gourds, herbs, and fragrant flowers that warm-climate gardeners can use, including plenty of hardy annuals suitable for mild-winter areas.

Park Seed Co.
Cokesbury Road
Greenwood, SC 29647-0001

All good gardeners must have Park's catalog, which includes carefully selected vegetable, flower, herb, and fruit varieties. The people at Park know how to pick winners.

Plants of the Southwest
Agua Fria
Rt. 6, Box 11-A
Santa Fe, NM 87501

Lots of native plants, plus vegetables, flowers, and fruits that will grow in the Southwest. The catalog is sure to give you a bad case of perennial fever.

Porter & Son
P.O. Box 104
Stephenville, TX 76410-0104

Extensive listings include old varieties that have become hard to find side by side with modern superhybrids that resist pests, diseases, and hot weather.

Redwood City Seed Co.
P.O. Box 361
Redwood City, CA 94064

Old varieties and a few new ones, including may unusual imports, all carefully trialed and taste tested. Catalog, $1.

Roswell Seed Co., Inc.
P.O. Box 925
Roswell, NM 88202

Most of the old standard vegetable varieties are sold here, along with seeds for cover crops, grasses, and grains. Bulk prices offered on many seeds.

Seeds*West
P.O. Box 1739
Elprado, NM 87529

Vegetable varieties selected for their flavor, beauty, and ability to grow in the Southwest. Flowers and herbs, too.

Shepherd's Garden Seeds

6116 Highway 9	30 Irene Street
Felton, CA 95018	Torrington, CT 06790

Consider many of this company's European vegetable varieties experimental, but trust the people at Shepherd's for carefully selected herbs, peppers, and flowers. The basil selection is without equal.

Southern Exposure Seed Exchange
P.O. Box 158
North Garden, VA 22959

Much careful study and observation goes into the selection of Southern Exposure's historical heirlooms and updated hybrids. A great source of onions, garlic, and southeastern specialties such as field peas and eggplant. Catalog, $3.

Southern Seeds
P.O. Box 2091
Melbourne, FL 32902

Vegetables that grow in semitropical areas, including hard-to-find Cuban squash, chayote, Seminole pumpkins, and a few selected fruits.

Stokes Seeds
P.O. Box 548
Buffalo, NY 14240

An extensive selection of vegetable varieties, many for cold climates and others unparalleled powerhouses of disease resistance. If you hear of something wonderful and new, Stokes may have it.

Tomato Growers Supply Co.
P.O. Box 2237
Fort Myers, FL 33902

The definitive source for tomatoes and peppers, both common and rare. More tomato varieties in one place than seed shoppers have ever known.

Westwind Seeds
2509 N. Campbell #139
Tucson, AZ 85719

Nonhybrid vegetables and herbs including regional specialties such as 'Tatume' squash and 'Numex' peppers.

Willhite Seed Co.
P.O. Box 23
Poolville, TX 76076

The melon marketplace for lovers of cantaloupes and watermelons.

ORNAMENTALS

Forestfarm
990 Tetherow Road
Williams, OR 97544

Sells more than a thousand species of trees, shrubs, flowers, and grasses as very young, and therefore affordable, plants. Catalog, $2.

Niche Gardens
1111 Dawson Road
Chapel Hill, SC 27516

Lovingly propagated perennials that can take heat, shipped in containers. Catalog, $3.

Wayside Gardens
1 Garden Lane
Hodges, SC 29695

Sophisticated ornamental plants, with price to match, for the discerning gardener. If you want a healthy rare shrub, you can trust Wayside.

FRUITS

States with fruit-breeding programs publish lists of area nurseries that propagate the latest university-bred varieties. Ask your Extension Service agent to get these lists for you. Many small nurseries do not sell through the mail, but the following nurseries do.

Bear Creek Nursery
P.O. Box 411
Northport, WA 99157

Native fruits are a specialty of Bear Creek, but this is a good place to find the best cultivars of rare small fruits, too.

Chestnut Hill Nursery
Rt. 1, Box 341
Alachua, FL 32615

Kaki persimmons and blight-resistant chestnuts are the house specialties, accompanied by a modest selection of figs and citrus fruits.

Edible Landscaping
P.O. Box 77
Afton, VA 22920

Propagates most of the major fruits you'd expect from a company with this name, plus unusual fall-fruiting cherries, Juneberries, and a number of figs. Some selections suitable only for cold-winter areas.

Hidden Springs Nursery
Rt. 14, Box 159
Cookeville, TN 38501

An odd selection of small, large, rare, and common fruits for edible landscapes, including some natives.

Ison's Nursery & Vineyard
Brooks, GA 30205

A muscadine marketplace, plus other fruits for the Southeast.

Northwoods Nursery
28696 S. Cramer Road
Molalla, OR 97038

Many hard-to-find and interesting fruits, shrubs, and trees. The selection of small fruits is outstanding.

Oregon Exotics
Rare Fruit Nursery
1065 Messenger Road
Grants Pass, OR 97527

This company specializes in "rare fruits for the North," but many warm-climate gardeners will be interested in the extensive selection of figs (more than twenty varieties) and other fruiting subtropicals.

Stark Brothers Nursery
Louisiana, MO 63353

America's leading name in backyard fruits meticulously selects varieties and sells expertly propagated plants.

WILDFLOWERS

Most of the general seed companies listed above sell wildflower seeds, but the following special sources are worthy of mention.

Clyde Robin Seed Co.
P.O. Box 2366
Castro Valley, CA 94546

Meadow wildflowers in abundance. The collection is extensive, with many suggestions for appropriate uses of various plants.

Wildseed, Inc.
P.O. Box 308
Eagle Lake, TX 77434

A great source for indigenous and naturalized wildflower seeds in small or large amounts, plus regional seed mixtures and a fine cultural guide.

INFORMATION ABOUT WILDFLOWERS

National Wildflower Research Center
2600 FM 973 North
Austin, TX 78725

Can tell you where to go in your state to buy nursery-propagated native wildflowers and rare plants. Also can furnish a list of wildflowers best adapted to your area, plus other special services related to wildflowers. Not a source of seeds.

SUPPLIES

Many seed companies also sell supplies, but the following companies specialize in garden supplies sold through the mail.

Gardener's Supply Co.
128 Intervale Road
Burlington, VT 05401

An interesting selection of supplies to make gardening and composting easier, plus some lovely decorative items for outdoor spaces.

Gardens Alive!
P.O. Box 149
Sunman, IN 47071

Unique ideas and products for waging a fight against bugs, along with fertilizers and unusual concoctions to help your soil work better.

Necessary Trading Company
P.O. Box 305
New Castle, VA 24127

If you can't find botanical pesticides, foliar fertilizers, or other organic supplies locally, call this company, the industry leader.

Walt Nicke Co.
P.O. Box 433
Topsfield, MA 01983

A large and varied selection of tools, including strange and common gardening aids.

BOOKS

In the middle of summer or the depths of winter, when the garden is quiet and your mind is hungry for new ideas, head to a library or bookstore and get your gardening batteries recharged. Libraries often have older books that can no longer be found in bookstores. Look for authors like Elizabeth Lawrence, Donald and Louise Hastings, and staff-produced books from *Southern Living* and *Sunset* magazines. I also love books by Texan William Welch, who always has something new in the works.

When selecting books, beware of those written by or for English gardeners. While no criticism of English gardeners is intended (they're the best in the world at gardening in England), much of the practical end of English gardening does not translate well to warm climates. Use British books for inspiration and thought enrichment, but go domestic when you want hard, reliable information.

Here are some of the best books I know for warm-climate gardeners who want to learn more.

The Complete Home Landscape Designer by Joel M. Lerner (New York: St. Martin's Press, 1992).

> *Trade tricks are explained, with visual aids such as punch-out templates and tear-out garden graphs. A wonderful guide for serious do-it-yourselfers.*

Desert Gardening by George Brookbank (Tuczon, AZ: Fisher Books, 1988).

If you want to plant a tree in Tucson, let Brookbank tell you how to do it. Also good advice on strawberries, cucurbits, and grapes.

Easy Garden Design by Janet Macunovich (Pownal, VT: Garden Way Publishing, 1992).

Step-by-step advice on how to create gardens and landscapes.

Growing and Propagating Wildflowers by Harry R. Phillips (Chapel Hill: University of North Carolina Press, 1985).

Especially valuable for gardeners willing to work patiently with native wild plants, with great information on propagation.

Herbaceous Perennial Plants by Allan Armitage (Athens, GA: Varsity Press, 1989).

If you feel like a lost soul venturing into the world of perennials, get this book to help unravel some of the mysteries.

Landscape Plants for the Southeast by Wade T. Batson (Columbia, SC: University of South Carolina Press, 1984).

Four hundred indigenous and introduced plants are identified, with uses and planting information included.

North American Horticulture, A Reference Guide by American Horticultural Society (New York: Charles Scribner's Sons, 1982).

A comprehensive guide to organizations of plant lovers (from bonsai to kiwi), American public gardens, horticultural libraries, and world records.

Secrets of Plant Propagation by Lewis Hill (Pownal, VT: Garden Way Publishing, 1985).

Information on how to start your own flowers, vegetables, fruits, berries, shrubs, trees, and houseplants.

Southern Herb Growing by Madalene Hill, Gwen Barclay, and Jean Hardy (Fredericksburg, TX: Shearer Publishing, 1987).

Expert firsthand information from Hilltop Herb Farm near Cleveland, Texas, is presented with good photos, great text, and fine recipes.

Square-Foot Gardening by Mel Bartholomew (Emmaus, PA: Rodale Press, 1981).

The classic guide for growing the most plants in the least space.

The Tropical Garden by William Warren and Luca I. Tettoni (New York and London: Thames & Hudson, 1991).

Lush photos of inspirational tropical gardens around the world.

Western Garden Book, 5th ed. by Sunset Magazine and Book Editors (Menlo Park, CA: Sunset Books, 1988).

If you live between Texas and Oregon, this is the first reference book you need. Includes a first-rate plant encyclopedia.

Wildflower Handbook by the National Wildflower Research Center (Austin, TX: Texas Monthly Press, 1989).

Includes a state-by-state list of botanical gardens, arboretums, and other places where native plants and wildflowers can be seen and appreciated, as well as sources for nursery-propagated native plants and wildflower seeds.

Woody Ornamentals for Deep South Gardens by David and Constance Rogers (Pensacola, FL: University of West Florida Press, 1991).

Exhaustive but academic guide to shrubs found in eastern sections of Zone 8.

KINDRED SPIRITS

If you're looking for a group that shares your horticultural passions, here are a handful of worthy candidates. When contacting them, write a short letter requesting membership information and enclose a self-addressed stamped envelope. Other organizations can be located through the book *North American Horticulture, A Reference Guide* (see page 198), which is available in many libraries (look in the reference section).

American Gourd Society
P.O. Box 274
Mount Gilead, OH 43338

American Rose Society
P.O. Box 30000
Shreveport, LA 71130

North American Fruit Explorers
Angling Road
Rt. 1, Box 50
PawPaw, IL 61353

Seed Savers Exchange
RR 3, Box 239
Decorah, IA 52101

World Pumpkin Confederation
14050 Gowanda State Road
Collins, NY 14034

USDA Hardiness Zone Map

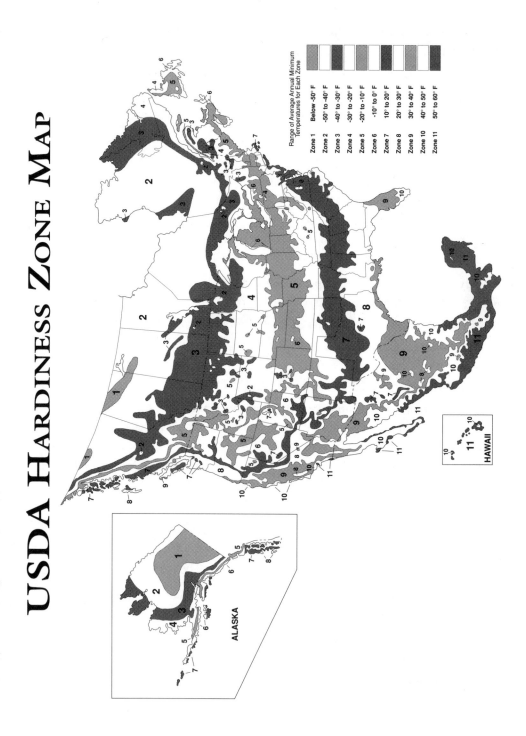

Range of Average Annual Minimum
Temperatures for Each Zone

Zone 1   Below -50° F
Zone 2   -50° to -40° F
Zone 3   -40° to -30° F
Zone 4   -30° to -20° F
Zone 5   -20° to -10° F
Zone 6   -10° to 0° F
Zone 7   0° to 10° F
Zone 8   10° to 20° F
Zone 9   20° to 30° F
Zone 10   30° to 40° F
Zone 11   40° to 50° F

HAWAII

ALASKA

INDEX

Page number in **boldface** refer to charts.
Page numbers in *italics* refer to illustrations.

Chickens, 25
Chilean bellflower. *See* Lapageria
Chinese cabbage, **51**, 52, 62, 72
Chinese forget-me-not *(Cynoglossum amabile)*, 141
Chives, 81
Chrysanthemum superbum. See Shasta daisy
Cilantro, 52
Citrus fruits, 117–118
Cobaea scandens. See Cup-and-saucer vine
Cold frame, 17, *17,* 35–37
Collard, **51**, 62. *See also* Brassicas
Columbine *(Aquilegia* species), 129
Companion planting, 28–29
Compost, 3–6, 53–54
  tea, 4, 185
Container planting, 146–147
Coreopsis *(Coreopsis* species), 129
Coriander, 52
Corn, 28, 48, 63, 72–73, *73*
Corn earworms, 168
Cortaderia selloana. See Pampas grass
Cover crops, 9–10, 44, 54–55
Cowpea cucurlios, 168
Crabgrass, 12
Cranberry, 120
Crocus, 140
Cucumber, 63, 73–74
Cucumber mosaic virus, 168, 186–187
Cucurbita species. *See* Gourd; Squash
Cucurbitaceae, 8
Cup-and-saucer vine *(Cobaea scandens),* 137
Curly top virus, 168, 187
Currant, 120
  golden *(Ribes aureum),* 112–113
Cutworms, 176
Cynoglossum amabile. See Chinese forget-me-not

Daffodil, 140, 160
Dahlia *(Dahlia* species), 129–130
Daikon radishes, 52
Daylilly *(Hemerocallis* species), 130
Design, garden, 122–124, 142–145
Dianthus *(Dianthus chinensis),* 59
Dianthus chinensis. See Dianthus
Dianthus deltoides. See Maiden pink
Diatomaceous earth, *171,* 178
Digitalis species. *See* Foxglove
Dill, 80
Disease resistance, 167–169
Dolichos lablab. See Hyacinth bean
Downy mildew, 168, 186
Drip irrigation, *41,* 67
Ducks, 25
Dusty miller *(Artemisia stellerana* and *Senecio cineraria),* 145

Early blight, 184
Echinacea purpurea. See Purple coneflower
Edging, 124
Eggplant, 63, 74–75
English ivy *(Hedera helix),* 161
Epimedium species, 162

Fall season, 50–55
  activity list, 55–57
Feijoa sellowiana. See Pineapple guava
Fennel, 62, 75–76
Fertilizing, 104, 139. *See also* Manure
Fescue, 154–155
  blue *(Festuca ovina glauca),* 158
Festuca ovina glauca. See Fescue, blue
Fig, 107–108
Fire ants, 176–177
Firewheel *(Gaillardia* species), 130–131
Fortunella, 118
Foundation plants, 123, *123*
Fountain grass *(Pennisetum alopecuroides),* 157
Four-o'clock *(Mirabilis* species), 131
Foxglove *(Digitalis* species), 141
Fungicides, natural, 115
Fusarium wilt, 168, 184

Gaillardia species. *See* Blanketflower; Firewheel
Garlic, 58, 63, 76
Garlic chives, 52, 140
Gay-feather *(Liatris* species), 131
Ginger, 76–77
Gladiolus, 140
Gooseberry, 120
Gourd, 63, 77–78, 137
Grafting, 75
Granite dust, 55
Grape, 108–109
Grass clippings, 7
Grasshoppers, 171, 177
Greens, 52, 62, 78–79, *79*
  See also specific greens
Greensand, 55
Gypsophila, 145
Gypsophila elegans. See Baby's-breath
Gypsum, 55

Harvesting, 42, 97–98
Heat-check, 42–43
Hedera helix. See English ivy
Hemerocallis species. *See* Daylilly
Hollyhock *(Althaea rosea),* 141
Hoop houses, 20–21, *21,* 47
Horticultural oil, 173
Houttuynia cordata. See Chameleon
Huckleberry, 106–107
Hyacinth bean *(Dolichos lablab),* 137
Hymenocallis, 140

Quaking grass *(Briza maxima), 157,* 158

Radish, 62, 88–89
Raspberry, 110
Rhubarb, 120
Ribbon grass *(Phalaris arundinacea),* 159
Ribes aureum. See Currant, golden
Rock phosphate, 55
Rose, 133
Rosemary, 81
Rotation, 8–9
Rotenone, 173–174, 178
Rudbeckia *(Rudbeckia* species), 133–134, *133*
Rye, annual, 155

Sabadilla, 173, 178
Sage, 58, 81
St. Augustine grass, 152
Salsify, 62, 89
Salt buildup, 10–12
Savory, 80
Scallion, 58, 62, 83
Schizachyrium scoparium. See Bluestem, little
Scilla, 140
Sedge *(Carex* species), 159
Sedum *(Sedum* species), 134
Seeds
   in compost, 5
   planting, 30–31, 34–36, *36,* 59–60, 78
   presprouting, 47
   suppliers, 190–194
Senecio cineraria. See Dusty miller
Shade, 19–21, 47–48
Shallot, 84
Shasta daisy *(Chrysanthemum superbum),* 59, 134
Shrubs, 55, 123, *123*
Silver grass, 157
Slat house, 19
Slugs, 178–179
Smut, 168
Snails, 178–179
Snapdragon, 59
Soap, insecticidal, 173
Soil, unimproved, 63
Solanaceae, 8
Solarization, soil, 182
Southern blight, 183–184
Spacing, plant, 69
Specimen plants, 124, *124*
Spider lilies *(Lyocoris radiata),* 140
Spider mites, 179
Spinach, 29, **51,** 58, 62, 89–90
Spring season, 34–38
   activity list, 38–40
Squash, 5, 63, 90–91
Squash borers, 70, 171, 179–180
Squash bugs, 70, 180

Stachys, 145–146
Statice, 59
Stock, 59
Strawberry, 58, 110-112, *111*
Succession cropping, 63
Sulfur, 10
Summer season, 40–47
   activity lists, 44–45, 49-50
Sunflower, 28, 48
Sunscald, 114
Supplies, mail order, 196–197
Sweet pea, 59
Sweet William, 59

Tansy, 28
Tarragon, 81
Texas root rot, 118, 183
Thunbergia alata. See Black-eyed Susan vine
Thyme, 81
Tobacco etch virus, 187
Tobacco mosaic virus, 168, 186–187
Tomatillo, 63, 92–93
Tomato, 5, 11–12, 19, 47, 63, 93–95
   heat-check, 43
   watering, 42
Tomato cages, 14, 54, 95
Tomato hornworms, 180
Tools, 13–15, *14*
Tulip, 140
Turnip, **51,** 62, 96

Umbelliferae, 8
Undercropping, 10
USDA hardiness zones, 1–2
   map, 200

Verbena *(Verbena* species), 134–135
Verticillium wilt, 168, 184
Vinca, 5, 146, 161
Vines, 136–138, *138,* 162
Viola species. *See* Pansy

Wallflower *(Cheiranthus* species), 59
Watering, 41, 47–49, 114
Watermelon, 63, 96–97
Weeds, 4, 11–13
White grubs, 168
White Nancy *(Lamium maculatum),* 162
Wildflowers, 135–136
   resources, 196
Winter season, 28–31
   activity list, 31–34
Wireworms, 168
Wisteria, 138

Yarrow *(Achillea* species), 135

Zoysia grass, 152